Teach Like the Mind Learns

OTHER BOOKS BY THIS AUTHOR

Fixing Instruction: Resolving Major Issues with a Core Body of Knowledge for Critical Instruction (2016)

Preparation for Critical Instruction: How to Explain Subject Matter While Teaching All Learners to Think, Read, and Write Critically (2016)

Teach Like the Mind Learns

Instruct So Students Learn to Think, Read, and Write Critically

Victor P. Maiorana

ROWMAN & LITTLEFIELD
Lanham • Boulder • New York • London

Published by Rowman & Littlefield
A wholly owned subsidiary of The Rowman & Littlefield Publishing Group, Inc.
4501 Forbes Boulevard, Suite 200, Lanham, Maryland 20706
www.rowman.com

Unit A, Whitacre Mews, 26-34 Stannary Street, London SE11 4AB

British Library Cataloguing in Publication Information Available

Library of Congress Cataloging-in-Publication Data Available

ISBN: 978-1-4758-2795-8 (cloth : alk. paper)
ISBN: 978-1-4758-2796-5 (pbk. : alk. paper)
ISBN: 978-1-4758-2797-2 (electronic)

∞™ The paper used in this publication meets the minimum requirements of American National Standard for Information Sciences—Permanence of Paper for Printed Library Materials, ANSI/NISO Z39.48-1992.

Printed in the United States of America

For Rosalie
Then, Now, and Forever

Contents

List of Figures xi

List of Tables xv

List of Text Boxes xvii

Preface xix

Acknowledgments xxiii

Introduction xxv

PART I: THE OPERATIONAL BASIS FOR CRITICAL INSTRUCTION

1 Fundamentals of Critical Instruction and Learning 3
Subject Matter Objective 3
Instructional Strategy, Technique, and Method 3
Subject Matter 5
Subject Matter Universals 5
Mind Grammar 6
Understand and Comprehend 6
Explain 7
Critical Thinking 7
Cogeracy 9
Critical Learning and Critical Instruction 10
Consequences of Mind Grammar–Based Assignments 10
Summary 12
Questions 12
Notes 12
Bibliography 14

2 The Mind Grammar Instructional Set 15
Subject Matter Objective 15
The Essence of Classroom Practice 15

What Is a Mind Grammar Instructional Set? 16
How to Develop and Use a Mind Grammar Instructional Set 16
Select a Specific Subject Matter Topic 17
Select a Critical Reasoning Strategy (MG1 or MG2) to Explain the Topic 17
Develop a Subject Matter Display 18
Design Classroom Assignments 21
Assemble, Use, Assess, and Revise the Instructional Set 24
Introducing Students to Critical Learning 26
Questions and Answers Regarding Critical Instruction Practice 26
The Consequences of Instructional Sets 34
Questions 35
Notes 35
Bibliography 36

3 Mind Grammar Instructional Techniques 37
Subject Matter Objective 37
Itechniques That Introduce Students to Critical Learning 38
Itechniques for Incomplete Subject Matter Displays 41
Itechniques for Critical Writing 42
Itechniques for Critical Reading 43
Itechniques for English Language Learners 46
Initial Itechniques for Students with Limited Skills 47
Itechniques for Problem Solving 49
Gamelike Itechniques 49
Itechniques for Collaboration 50
Still Deeper Learning through Exploratory Itechniques 52
Creative Thinking Itechniques 53
Computer-Based Itechniques 54
Instructional Techniques and Mind Grammar Vocabulary 55
Questions 56
Notes 56
Bibliography 57

PART II: THE PRACTICE OF CRITICAL INSTRUCTION

4 Instructional Sets for the English Language Arts 61
Subject Matter Objective 61
Let's Explore the Story of Jack and Jill 61
Let's Explore Further the Story of Jack and Jill 64
Introduction to Critical Learning 65
Introduction to Critical Learning for English Language Learners 66
The Adverb 68
Lincoln's Gettysburg Address in Spanish 70
Critical Visualization 72
Additional Teacher Resources 73
Application Assignments 78
Bibliography 79

5 Instructional Sets for the Humanities 81
Subject Matter Objective 81
A Wild Style of Painting 81
The Painting *Big Ben* by Andre Derain 84
Music 87
Listen to a Poem 89
The Battle of Gettysburg 90
Lincoln's Gettysburg Address in English 92
Additional Teacher Resources 94
Application Assignments 96
Note 98
Bibliography 98

6 Instructional Sets for Mathematics, Science, Engineering, and Technology 99
Subject Matter Objective 99
The Circle 100
Percentages 102
Probability 104
Subscripted Variables 105
Geography 107
Electrically Charged Clouds 109
An Immunization Experiment 110
Ohm's Law of Electricity 112
The Cell Phone 114
Additional Teacher Resources 116
Applications Assignments 120
Notes 122
Bibliography 123

7 Instructional Sets for the Social Sciences 125
Subject Matter Objective 125
The First Amendment to the Constitution of the United States 125
An Economic System 128
Economists 131
The Declaration of Independence 132
Credit Information Agencies 133
Additional Teacher Resources 135
Application Assignments 138
Bibliography 140

Glossary 143

Index 149

About the Author 155

List of Figures

CHAPTER 4: INSTRUCTIONAL SETS FOR THE ENGLISH LANGUAGE ARTS

Figure 4.1 The Story of Jack and Jill 61
Figure 4.2 A Subject Matter Display of the Story of Jack and Jill 63
Figure 4.3 A Subject Matter Display of Rain (Blank) 66
Figure 4.4 A Four-Stage MG2 Subject Matter Display of the Adverb 69
Figure 4.5 Una Visualizacion de la Materia del Discurso de Lincoln en Gettysburg 1863 71–72
Figure 4.6 A Four-Stage MG2 Subject Matter Display of the Three Modes of Critical Thinking 74–75
Figure 4.7 A Four-Stage MG2 Subject Matter Display of Reading for Critical Comprehension 75–76
Figure 4.8 A Four-Stage MG2 Subject Matter Display of the Writing Plan for Critical Explanation 76
Figure 4.9 A Three-Stage MG1 Subject Matter Display of Herman the Horse 77
Figure 4.10 A Three-Stage MG2 Subject Matter Display of the Comma 77
Figure 4.11 A Four-Stage MG2 Subject Matter Display of a Library (Compressed) 79

CHAPTER 5: INSTRUCTIONAL SETS FOR THE HUMANITIES

Figure 5.1 A Wild Style of Painting 82
Figure 5.2 A Three-Stage MG1 Subject Matter Display of the Fauve Painting Style 83
Figure 5.3 A Three-Stage MG2 Subject Matter Display of Andre Derain's Painting *Big Ben* 86
Figure 5.4 A Two-Stage MG1 Subject Matter Display of Music 87
Figure 5.5 A Four-Stage MG2 Subject Matter Display of Music 88

Figure 5.6 A Four-Stage MG2 Subject Matter Display of the Battle of Gettysburg from the North's Point of View 91
Figure 5.7 A Four-Stage MG2 Subject Matter Display of Lincoln's Gettysburg Address of 1863 94
Figure 5.8 A Four-Stage MG2 Subject Matter Display of Perspective in Drawing 94–95
Figure 5.9 A Four-Stage MG2 Subject Matter Display of Philosophy 95

CHAPTER 6: INSTRUCTIONAL SETS FOR MATHEMATICS, SCIENCE, ENGINEERING, AND TECHNOLOGY

Figure 6.1 A Three-Stage MG2 Subject Matter Display of the Circle 101
Figure 6.2 A Four-Stage MG2 Subject Matter Display of Probability 105
Figure 6.3 A Four-Stage MG2 Subject Matter Display of Geography 108
Figure 6.4 A Two-Stage MG1 Subject Matter Display of Electrically Charged Clouds 109
Figure 6.5 A Four-Stage MG2 Subject Matter Display of Electrically Charged Clouds 110
Figure 6.6 A Two-Stage MG1 Subject Matter Display of the Cell Phone 115
Figure 6.7 The Consequences of Cell Phone Use 115
Figure 6.8 A Four-Stage MG2 Subject Matter Display of Counting (Compressed) 116
Figure 6.9 A Four-Stage MG2 Subject Matter Display of the Human Digestive System (Compressed) 116
Figure 6.10 A Three-Stage MG2 Subject Matter Display of the Large Intestine 117
Figure 6.11 A Four-Stage MG2 Subject Matter Display of Litmus Paper 117
Figure 6.12 A Four-Stage MG2 Subject Matter Display of Ethical Drugs for Human Use 118
Figure 6.13 A Four-Stage MG2 Subject Matter Display of the Engineering Design for the Apollo Program's Lunar Module Electrical Storage Batteries 119

CHAPTER 7: INSTRUCTIONAL SETS FOR THE SOCIAL SCIENCES

Figure 7.1 A Four-Stage MG2 Subject Matter Display of the First Amendment to the Constitution of the United States 127
Figure 7.2 A Four-Stage MG2 Subject Matter Display of an Economic System (Incomplete) 129
Figure 7.3 A Four-Stage MG2 Subject Matter Display of an Economic System (Complete) 130

Figure 7.4	A Four-Stage MG2 Subject Matter Display of the United States Declaration of Independence, Adopted on July 4, 1776	133
Figure 7.5	Out-of-Order Credit Activities	134
Figure 7.6	A Four-Stage MG2 Subject Matter Display of Credit Information Agencies	135
Figure 7.7	A Three-Stage MG2 Subject Matter Display of Bloom's Taxonomy of Educational Objectives—Book I Cognitive Domain	136
Figure 7.8	A Two-Stage MG1 Subject Matter Display of Maslow's Theory of Human Needs	137
Figure 7.9	A Two-Stage MG1 Subject Matter Display of a Typical American Business	137
Figure 7.10	A Four-Stage MG2 Subject Matter Display of Martin Luther King Jr.'s "I Have a Dream" Speech	137

List of Tables

CHAPTER 2: THE MIND GRAMMAR INSTRUCTIONAL SET

Table 2.1 Assignment Assessment Factors 25

CHAPTER 4: INSTRUCTIONAL SETS FOR THE ENGLISH LANGUAGE ARTS

Table 4.1 Examples of Consequences 64
Table 4.2 Critical Learning Terms Translation Table 66
Table 4.3 The Hand Translation Table 67

CHAPTER 5: INSTRUCTIONAL SETS FOR THE HUMANITIES

Table 5.1 Activities 82
Table 5.2 Resources 83
Table 5.3 The Battle of Gettysburg from the North's Point of View 90

CHAPTER 7: INSTRUCTIONAL SETS FOR THE SOCIAL SCIENCES

Table 7.1 Some Mind Grammar Elements of an Economic System 128

List of Text Boxes

CHAPTER 1: FUNDAMENTALS OF CRITICAL INSTRUCTION AND LEARNING

Text Box 1.1	The Three Modes of Critical Thinking	8
Text Box 1.2	Cogeracy: The Mind's Palette—The Four Categories of Thinking	9

CHAPTER 2: THE MIND GRAMMAR INSTRUCTIONAL SET

Text Box 2.1	Procedure to Develop and Use an Instructional Set	16
Text Box 2.2	How to Develop a Subject Matter Display	20–21

CHAPTER 4: INSTRUCTIONAL SETS FOR THE ENGLISH LANGUAGE ARTS

Text Box 4.1	How It Rains	65
Text Box 4.2	The Adverb	68
Text Box 4.3	Discurso Gettysburg de Lincoln	70

CHAPTER 5: INSTRUCTIONAL SETS FOR THE HUMANITIES

Text Box 5.1	Lincoln's Gettysburg Address	92

CHAPTER 6: INSTRUCTIONAL SETS FOR MATHEMATICS, SCIENCE, ENGINEERING, AND TECHNOLOGY

Text Box 6.1	Percentages	102–103
Text Box 6.2	Subscripted Variables	106
Text Box 6.3	An Immunization Experiment	111–112
Text Box 6.4	Ohm's Law of Electricity	113

CHAPTER 7: INSTRUCTIONAL SETS FOR THE SOCIAL SCIENCES

Text Box 7.1	First Amendment to the Constitution of the United States	126
Text Box 7.2	A Narrative on the First Amendment	127
Text Box 7.3	Job Title: Economist	131

Preface

As a human being, you possess an awe-inspiring gift. You were born with it. The gift is the ability to reason critically. Your conscious mind has its own innate, informal, grammar (i.e., system, pattern) for thinking critically. You get better at critical thinking as you live and experience life.

Your grammar of mind always seeks intent, identifies the activities needed to achieve intent, and when thinking fully, considers the consequences that follow. This is how the mind works. This is how the mind learns. You use this critical mind grammar pattern repeatedly throughout the day. However, it is used informally.

This means our innate ability to think critically is not readily applied to curriculum subject matter. It is not applied in explicit, formal, and reproducible ways that can be taught to and learned by others. For this to happen, in teacher preparation and professional development programs, in school and college classrooms, and in educational materials, innate critical thinking must be made more explicit, formal, and developed. Such thinking is called mind grammar.

To think, read, and write critically of anything, including the subject matter taught and studied in schools and colleges, a formal critical reasoning process is required. The process involves first establishing the *subject matter's* intent and then showing how that intent is achieved and with what consequences. Mind grammar, originated by your author, makes it possible to explain subject matter critically and formally so it is readily understood and comprehended. Because it represents a fundamental critical reasoning process, mind grammar also provides the means to read and write critically.

My work *Fixing Instruction: Resolving Major Issues with a Core Body of Knowledge for Critical Instruction* (2016) establishes, for the first time, the basis on which to found the professional practice of critical instruction. This was followed by *Preparation for Critical Instruction: How to Explain Subject Matter While Teaching All Learners to Think, Read, and Write Critically* (2016), which establishes how to learn critically so one is prepared to teach critically.

Teach Like the Mind Learns takes the core body of knowledge for critical instruction introduced in *Fixing Instruction*, and fully developed in *Preparation for Critical Instruction*, and applies it to the design of critically conceived classroom assignments.

This book shows how to design assignments for school and college classrooms so you may practice critical instruction through the formal application of mind grammar.

This book is important for the following reasons:

- It calls on and develops the human being's innate but informal gift to think critically. It applies the gift formally. This allows all teachers to instruct and all students to learn in ways that develop language arts abilities in critical thinking, reading, listening, writing, speaking, and observing when engaging new and revisited subject matter.
- All learners, including disadvantaged, English language learner, and general and special education students, possess the innate gift to reason critically. This book shows how to maximize that gift regardless of a student's background and state of readiness.
- It shows how to develop instructional sets. An instructional set is a collection of classroom assignments designed to instruct critically so your students can learn critically. The assignments lead students to learn to think, read, listen, write, speak, and observe critically as the means to understand and comprehend subject matter.
- A variety of across-discipline instructional sets provide examples of how to apply mind grammar to new and revisited subject matter.
- Teacher resources are provided within each instructional set. Resources can include a subject matter display, which provides a critical view of a given topic; critically written narratives; other materials; references; and notes on how to use the assignments in the classroom. Additional teacher resources are provided at the end of each chapter.

With this book you will learn to do the following:

- Teach like the mind learns.
- Introduce critical learning to your elementary through college students.
- Share, with elementary through college students, your core knowledge of critical thinking, reading, and writing in an explicit, clear, and transparent manner. Students will become your active cognitive partners in the acts of education.
- Design classroom assignments based on the mind's innate ability to reason critically.
- Apply critical reasoning patterns, referred to as MG1 and MG2, to the design of classroom assignments that engage students critically in the six language arts.
- Design classroom assignments based on pairing mind grammar instructional strategy with a variety of over ninety, mostly student-centered, instructional techniques.

Teach Like the Mind Learns is meant for use as a textbook in teacher preparation and professional development programs. It is meant for practicing faculty to bring critical instruction and learning into their classrooms. It is written primarily for teacher educators, teacher-candidates, school and college faculty, principals, assistant principals, and professional developers. With this book, the teaching profession now has explicit across-discipline examples of how to meet the school, college, workplace, and citizen needs of life in the digital twenty-first century.

The main consequences of this book are greatly improved teacher preparation and practice and student learning. Disadvantaged, English language learner, and general and special education students will have their innate abilities to reason critically nurtured and developed. This will lead to significantly improved achievement of all students at all levels.

By merging subject matter instruction with the development of critical language arts abilities, the professional practice of all faculty and the achievement of all students will be substantially more tangible, respected, and universally prized.

Acknowledgments

I thank Catherine Alfieri; Sandra C. Hassan; Louis Barella; John Black; Michael Bronner, PhD; Vincent B. Ciofalo, PhD; Marietta Cleckley; Thomas B. Colwell Jr., PhD; Louis Deluca, EdD; Anthony DeMaio; Donna Dirico; Barbara V. Dunne; Dolores Edwards; Susan Field; Albert Forte; Stanley Gartenberg; Louis E. Guida Jr., MD; Fiona Hughes-McDonnell, EdD; Charles A. Keenan; Freda Kolinsky; Ann C. Maiorana; Janet Mascoll; Edward E. Miller; Michael F. Miller; Jennifer Mingione, MD; Victoria Rose Mingione; Morton A. Ostrowsky; William Ringle; Murray V. Romano; Daphne A. Sabella; Padmakar M. Sapre, PhD; Herbert S. Siegel; Kate Smith; Sidney Sonsky; Alexandria Tarasko; Susan Traub; and Joseph A. Volker, PhD. The advice of Dr. Tom Koerner, vice president of education at Rowman & Littlefield, has helped greatly in this writing project. I thank Carlie Wall, associate editorial editor, Kayla Riddleberger, associate production editor, and copyeditor Erin Cler for their most effective work.

Introduction

Teach Like the Mind Learns: *Instruct So Students Learn to Think, Read, and Write Critically* shows how to instruct in ways that are natural to the critically disposed human mind. Such instructional practice, referred to as critical instruction, is the explicit and critical explanation of how to connect and integrate the objectives, processes, and consequences within subject matter. It is practiced in ways that concurrently develop abilities in critical thinking, reading, listening, writing, speaking, and observing in all students.

This work is the third in a series of books on critical instruction. The first, *Fixing Instruction: Resolving Major Issues with a Core Body of Knowledge for Critical Instruction*, establishes for the profession a core body of knowledge for critical instruction. It provides a language of instruction, shows why conventional serialism-based instruction is self-defeating for both teachers and students, draws on the human being's innate critical grammar of mind as the foundation for critical instruction and learning, outlines a critical instruction curriculum for teacher preparation programs, and gives a foundation for developing long-missing standards for thinking, the first language art.

The second work, *Preparation for Critical Instruction: How to Explain Subject Matter While Teaching All Learners to Think, Read, and Write Critically*, expands on the core body of knowledge provided by *Fixing Instruction*. It explains the nature, theory, and principles of subject matter; demonstrates the mind's innate but informal ability to think critically and formally applies that natural ability in the form of mind grammar to engage subject matter in all disciplines; develops the concept of cogeracy, which addresses the four categories of conscious thinking—recall, logical, critical, and creative thinking; shows how to use mind grammar reasoning strategies to explicitly and critically read for critical comprehension and write for critical explanation; and introduces the design of classroom assignments that engage students in the six language arts.

This brings us to the present book. *Teach Like the Mind Learns* fully develops how to design and use classroom assignments that pair mind grammar instructional strategies with instructional techniques. End-of-chapter questions and application assignments are included in each chapter. The book is organized in two parts.

PART I: THE OPERATIONAL BASIS FOR CRITICAL INSTRUCTION

Part I discusses the operational basis for critical instruction. Chapters in part I provide the fundamentals of critical instruction, how to develop a mind grammar–based instructional set, and a great variety of instructional techniques for use in designing classroom assignments.

Chapter 1, Fundamentals of Critical Instruction and Learning, begins with a discussion of an essential part of teacher preparation and practice: an understanding of key professional terms and concepts. This means, for example, an understanding of what major terms such as strategy, technique, and method mean instructionally. It means understanding what is meant by concepts such as critical thinking, reading, and writing and critical understanding, comprehension, and explanation.

Beyond that, it means understanding the processes associated with critical instruction and how they factor into the development and use of classroom assignments. This provides the basis for the design of critically based classroom assignments. Such assignments lead students to engage new and revisited subject matter while concurrently developing their ability to think, read, listen, write, speak, and observe critically.

Chapter 2, The Mind Grammar Instructional Set, describes how to develop and use an instructional set. An instructional set is a collection of classroom assignments that address a specific subject matter topic. The assignments use instructional techniques with mind grammar as the instructional strategy. There are two mind grammar strategies for explaining subject matter: MG1 achieves understanding, and MG2 achieves comprehension.

The procedure for developing an instructional set is described. It includes selecting a specific subject matter topic, selecting a mind grammar critical reasoning strategy to use for explaining the topic, and developing a subject matter display. Text Box 2.2 provides guidelines for developing a subject matter display. Described are the different types of classroom assignments that may be included in a set. They are reasoning, reading, listening, writing, speaking, observing, application, and homework assignments. Table 2.1 contains a series of factors to consider when assessing the classroom use of the assignments within an instructional set. Next discussed are informal and formal ways to introduce students to critical learning.

The chapter includes a section of special interest. Included are seventeen questions and answers regarding the practice of critical instruction. The first question is, Why can't teacher–educators, school and college faculty, and professional developers continue to instruct the way they always have? The second question is, So serialism-induced rote learning is of little or no value? Other questions address using mind grammar in special education, blended, and English language learner classes; learning styles; and whether one must first know something about a subject matter topic before being asked to think critically of it.

The chapter concludes with a discussion of the consequences of using mind grammar–based instructional sets for teacher–educators, teacher-candidates, practicing teachers, and professional developers.

Chapter 3, Mind Grammar Instructional Techniques, describes many ways to design assignments that actively engage students critically with subject matter. Classroom assignments that produce critical thinking, reading, and writing need two key resources: first, an instructional strategy based on a critical reasoning strategy, and second, an instructional technique that is paired with the critical reasoning strategy. That combination yields a critical instructional method. Using mind grammar as the instructional strategy, over ninety itechniques distributed among twelve categories are presented.

The categories are Itechniques That Introduce Students to Critical Learning, Itechniques for Incomplete Subject Matter Displays, Itechniques for Critical Writing, Itechniques for Critical Reading, Itechniques for English Language Learners, Itechniques for Students with Limited Skills, Itechniques for Problem Solving, Gamelike Itechniques, Itechniques for Collaboration, Still Deeper Learning through Exploratory Itechniques, Creative Thinking Itechniques, and Computer-Based Itechniques.

Most itechniques require students to work at thinking, reading, and writing critically. This leaves you free to provide help to individuals or groups as needed. Most all itechniques lend themselves to group work.

The itechniques represent an ever-enlarging collection. You can adapt, revise, modify, or improve the itechniques as desired. Better still, you can create your own itechniques.

PART II: THE PRACTICE OF CRITICAL INSTRUCTION

Chapters in part II illustrate how to develop instructional sets on topics in the English language arts; the humanities; mathematics, science, engineering, and technology; and the social sciences. Each set contains a number of classroom assignments as well as teacher resources. The resources contain guides for using the assignments in class. Each chapter contains a section on Additional Teacher Resources, which provides the basis for designing instructional sets on a variety of topics. Application Assignments appear at the end of each chapter.

Chapter 4, Instructional Sets for the English Language Arts, includes instructional sets on Let's Explore the Story of Jack and Jill, Let's Explore Further the Story of Jack and Jill, Introduction to Critical Learning, The Adverb, Introducing Critical Learning to English Language Learners, Lincoln's Gettysburg Address in Spanish, and Critical Visualization. The chapter section Additional Teacher Resources contains subject matter displays on critical thinking, critical reading, critical writing, reading an editorial, Herman the Horse, and the comma.

Chapter 5, Instructional Sets for the Humanities, includes instructional sets on A Wild Style of Painting, The Painting *Big Ben* by Andre Derain, Music, Listen to a Poem, The Battle of Gettysburg, and Lincoln's Gettysburg Address in English. The chapter section Additional Teacher Resources contains subject matter displays on philosophy and perspective in drawing.

Chapter 6, Instructional Sets for Mathematics, Science, Engineering, and Technology, includes instructional sets on the circle, percentages, probability, subscripted variables, geography, electrically charged clouds, an immunization experiment, Ohm's Law of electricity, and the cell phone. The chapter section Additional Teacher Resources contains subject matter displays or narratives on counting, the digestive system, the large intestine, litmus paper, ethical drugs, and the electrical batteries used on the Apollo program's Lunar Module, the spaceship that landed men on the moon.

Chapter 7, Instructional Sets for the Social Sciences, includes instructional sets on The First Amendment to the Constitution of the United States, An Economic System, Economists, The Declaration of Independence, and credit information agencies. The chapter section Additional Teacher Resources contains subject matter displays on Bloom's Taxonomy of Educational Objectives—Book I Cognitive Domain, Maslow's Theory of Human Needs, a typical American business, and Martin Luther King Jr.'s "I Have a Dream" speech.

With *Teach Like the Mind Learns*, teacher–educators, teacher-candidates, school and college faculty, principals, assistant principals, superintendents, education school and faculty deans, and professional developers now have the basis to overcome a long-standing and self-imposed disadvantage. Your best efforts will no longer be thwarted by self-defeating serialism-based instruction.

With mind grammar, you will teach in ways that all learners are innately disposed to learn. You will teach like the mind learns.

BIBLIOGRAPHY

Maiorana, V. P. (2016). *Fixing instruction: Resolving major issues with a core body of knowledge for critical instruction.* Lanham, MD: Rowman & Littlefield.

Maiorana, V. P. (2016). *Preparation for critical instruction: How to explain subject matter while teaching all learners to think, read, and write critically.* Lanham, MD: Rowman & Littlefield.

Part I

THE OPERATIONAL BASIS FOR CRITICAL INSTRUCTION

Chapter One

Fundamentals of Critical Instruction and Learning

Subject Matter Objective: The purpose of critical instruction and learning is to explain new and revisited subject matter critically to all students while at the same time developing their ability to think, read, listen, write, speak, and observe critically.

A necessary part of professional teacher preparation and practice is an understanding of key terms and concepts. This means, for example, an understanding of what terms such as strategy, technique, and method mean instructionally. It means understanding what is meant by concepts such as critical thinking, reading, and writing and critical understanding, comprehension, and explanation.

Beyond that, it means understanding the processes associated with critical instruction[1] and how they factor into the development and use of classroom assignments. In this chapter[2] we discuss the major terms and concepts associated with the practice of critical instruction. This provides the basis for the design of critically based classroom assignments. Such assignments lead students to engage new and revisited subject matter while concurrently developing their ability to think, read, listen, write, speak, and observe critically.

INSTRUCTIONAL STRATEGY, TECHNIQUE, AND METHOD

As related to teacher preparation and instructional practice, the terms *strategy*, *technique*, and *method* should not be moving targets.[3] To be clear, precise, and effective *within the profession* the word "instructional" should precede each term. So instructionally, the terms become *instructional strategy*, *instructional technique*, and *instructional method*. Here are definitions of the new terms.

Descriptions of Instructional Strategies, Techniques, and Methods

An Instructional Strategy (Istrategy)

Of the three key terms, istrategy is discussed first because it provides the premise, the reasoning foundation, for how you choose to think of subject matter.

An instructional strategy is the mental view one takes of subject matter. Istrategy is how one reasons when thinking of new and revisited subject matter.[4] An explicit istrategy is *arranging subject matter* according to some *reasoning framework* or thinking theory for purposes of understanding, comprehending, and explaining subject matter.

Said another way, an istrategy provides the basis of how you choose to have your mind arrange (i.e., organize, systemize, assemble, construct, form patterns for) *subject matter* when you think, read, and write.[5] It is therefore the mental foundation for how you ask your students to think, read, and write when seeking to promote their understanding and comprehension of subject matter.

An Instructional Technique (Itechnique)

An instructional technique provides the means to implement an istrategy. An itechnique is a way to actively engage students *with the subject matter at hand.* All itechniques are used in the context of some explicit istrategy.

An Instructional Methodology (Imethod)

An instructional methodology is a combination of a specific istrategy and a specific itechnique for *engaging subject matter*. One selects a specific istrategy and merges it with a specific itechnique to form a specific imethod.

Examples of Istrategies, Itechniques, and Imethods

Examples of Istrategies

Serialism is the teaching profession's weak default instructional strategy used in teacher preparation programs, classroom instruction, tutoring programs, and professional development programs. It is how subject matter is treated in textbooks, instructional software, Internet pages, and other forms of subject matter delivery.

Serialism istrategy is the strictly linear and traditional mental view of subject matter. It reveals little with respect to how all subject matter is universally constructed, connected, and integrated.

Serialism istrategy is the discussion of subject matter topics one after another without also making and revealing critical connections within and among the topics. Because it provides no critical pattern for subject matter engagement, serialism-based instruction induces rote learning and defeats the concurrent development of critical thinking, reading, and writing abilities. For further discussion of serialism-based instruction, see Chapter 2, Instructional Practice Is Inherently Weak: The Hidden Story, in *Fixing Instruction* (Maiorana, 2016a).

There are critical ways to engage subject matter. These include strategies such as ends-means, effect-cause, and mind grammar. Mind grammar is more cognitively powerful than the first two because it integrates, expands, and extends their effectiveness. This provides the basis for critical understanding, comprehension, and explanation of subject matter when thinking, reading, and writing.

Examples of Itechniques

Group work, case study, role-play, debate, field trips, simulations, team teaching, do nows, mapping, question for recall, KWL (know, want to know, have learned), writing in the content areas, close reading, and recitation[6] are all examples of itechniques.

Itechniques are of limited critical instructional and learning value if the underlying instructional thinking strategy is weak. The best technique for measuring the size of a person's head will lead nowhere if employed in the service of a strategy or theory that holds that intellectual ability is related to head size.

Examples of Imethods

We are now able to assemble an imethod. Pairing serialism istrategy with the itechnique of mapping assignments is an imethod. Similarly, *pairing* serialism istrategy with a do-now handout, or group work, or recitation, or with any itechnique represents an imethod. But be aware that any itechnique that is paired with serialism is fundamentally flawed as an instructional method. Pairing mind grammar with a writing or reading itechnique is an imethod that develops critical language abilities.

No technique can or does alter cognitive strategy. So keep in mind that *it is not* the wide variety of traditional and favored itechniques that creative teachers have developed and used over the years that make instructional practice weak. It is the underlying reasoning strategy used when engaging new and revisited subject matter. That is what mainly determines the extent of teacher effectiveness and student achievement.

SUBJECT MATTER

Anything you can think about is subject matter. Anything you can read, write, talk about, or imagine is subject matter. Subject matter is anything you believe. Subject matter is anything on earth and beyond. Subject matter is all that has gone before, exists now, or will exist in the future.

SUBJECT MATTER UNIVERSALS

Subject matter is composed of the ideas, concepts, theories, facts, and processes ever discovered, conceived, imagined, revealed, believed, and thought of by the human mind. There is a universal composition to subject matter. It contains the attributes of subject matter objective, processes, and consequences. The most important of these attributes is the subject matter objective. A subject matter objective is the explicit end-in-view, effect, meaning, importance, purpose, *or* function of the *subject matter topic* at hand.[7]

The attributes are shared by all topics in all disciplines. The attributes can be arranged systematically in a universal critical pattern. Subject matter is the product of the human mind, and so it reflects how the mind operates. With mind grammar, one can reveal the universal and critical nature that is within all subject matter.

MIND GRAMMAR

Mind grammar[8] is the innate, systematic, and patterned way that the human mind encounters the world and all its subject matter. It is a natural system of thinking that provides the basis for critical learning, which is the basis for critical instruction. Innate mind grammar is the basis for understanding, comprehending, and explaining subject matter.

Mind grammar reasoning patterns reveal, connect, and integrate the objectives, processes, and consequences universally present within all subject matter. Two reasoning patterns are used and referred to as MG1 and MG2. They provide the foundation to critically explain something to oneself (self-instruction) or to others (critical instruction). Critical instruction is professional practice that achieves understanding and comprehension of subject matter in students in ways that develop their critical thinking, reading, and writing abilities.

UNDERSTAND AND COMPREHEND

The Merriam-Webster dictionary defines *understand* as "to achieve a grasp of the nature, significance, or explanation of something."

A definition of *comprehend* is "To contain or hold within a total scope, significance . . . the truth of everything which . . . (one) may understand." *Comprehensive* is further described as "covering completely . . . having or exhibiting wide mental grasp."

The Two Terms in Daily Life

In our conscious daily life, we frequently, if not always, first identify our intentions and then act on them. Many of our intentions become implicit (e.g., to clean our teeth, to get dressed, to attend classes, to go to work) and so become habits. To act on these intentions, we brush our teeth, dress, and travel to class or work.

Other intentions are explicit (e.g., buy toothpaste, replace an old pair of shoes, and arrange a special meeting). To act on these intentions, we travel to stores or visit the Internet and make purchases. In the case of a meeting, activities include establishing an agenda and identifying a meeting time and place.

So if we were to follow ourselves around, we would understand that certain actions (processes) are taking place (e.g., brushing one's teeth), be*cause* they are needed to achieve some *effect* (e.g., clean teeth). Notice that our daily actions are preceded by intent, which causes the actions. In other words, intent is the same as seeking some effect. The actions related to the effect cause the effect to be achieved.

We may say then that to understand is to recognize an effect-cause or ends-means relationship. To comprehend is to recognize deeply the consequences that can follow such relationships.

The Two Terms in Instructional Practice

Here are how the two terms may be framed for use as instructional strategies. To understand is to focus on the intent and processes of a subject matter topic. To comprehend goes further and considers the significance (the consequences) of the topic.

So achieving understanding of subject matter requires a first level of critical thinking. This is called Mind Grammar One (MG1). It takes the form of intent-process. Achieving comprehension of subject matter requires a deeper and more thoughtful second level of critical thinking. This is called Mind Grammar Two (MG2). It takes the form of intent-process-consequences. Both these thinking strategies provide the reasoning basis for critical learning, which in turn is the basis for critical instruction (i.e., explanation).

EXPLAIN

Describing subject matter is not the same as explaining it. For example, a toothbrush can be described as a small brush attached to a long handle. Sneakers can be described as foot covers secured through laces. Neither of these descriptions explicitly addresses the intent, activities, or consequences associated with a toothbrush or sneakers.

As Vygotsky (1976) observed, describing is not explaining because "Mere description does not reveal the actual dynamic relations [e.g., effect-cause, ends-means, intent-activities-consequences] that underlie phenomena" (p. 62). Said another way, to explain is "To give a reason for . . . [and] show the . . . development [and] relationship[s] of [some topic]" (*Merriam-Webster's*, 2007, p. 440).

If one's aim is to explain, one must go beyond describing content serially[9] and engage in critical thinking for comprehension. One might assume that graphic organizers can serve as the basis for critical explanation (i.e., critical instruction). However, graphic organizers are only serially descriptive, they do not represent a critical reasoning strategy.

Because of their serial nature, graphic organizers cannot develop critical understanding and comprehension of subject matter. Furthermore, they provide no mental basis for critical reading and writing. As presently practiced, they are not supported by a critical theory of subject matter, such as subject matter universals. They lack a thinking strategy that reveals that criticality, such as mind grammar.[10]

To give a reason for a topic's existence and show its development and relationships requires an explicit critical reasoning strategy. Mind grammar provides that strategy. Accordingly, critical explanation is showing explicitly the connection and integration of the objectives, processes, and consequences associated with the subject matter topic at hand.

CRITICAL THINKING

The Three Modes of Critical Thinking

Among educators and the general population, critical thinking tends to be thought of, discussed, and written about as if problem solving covered all aspects of critical thinking. However, there are three modes of critical thinking. Therefore, it is important to distinguish and understand the three modes. This will provide substance and clarity when discussing, reading, and writing of the nature and application of critical thinking.

The three modes (and purposes) of critical thinking are subject matter understanding/comprehension/explanation, argumentation, and problem solving.[11] To argue is to present one's view on an issue or to debate another on the issue. It includes the use of probing questions to reveal weaknesses in another's position (e.g., the Socratic method) and argument mapping. Approaches to problem solving include the problem-solving method and the scientific method.

Effective argumentation and problem solving require that *one first comprehend critically* the subject matter topic at hand. This requires knowing how to explicitly think, read, and write for critical comprehension when engaging new and revisited subject matter. However, preparing teachers to explain new and revisited subject matter critically has long been missing from teacher preparation and professional development programs. Therefore, critical practice has also long been missing from classrooms at all levels.[12]

Text Box 1.1 summarizes the three modes of critical thinking.

Text Box 1.1

THE THREE MODES OF CRITICAL THINKING

Critical thinking strategies for (1) understanding, comprehending, and explaining subject matter; (2) argumentation; and (3) problem solving.

1. Subject matter reasoning strategies for understanding and comprehension (learning) and explanation (instruction)

To explicitly analyze, synthesize, and evaluate the universal elements present in new and revisited subject matter through use of MG1 and MG2 mind grammar. MG1 and MG2 provide the basis for (a) critical understanding and critical comprehension of new and revisited subject matter in one's self (critical learning) and (b) explicit instructional strategies for explaining subject matter to all students through the design of student-centered classroom assignments (critical instruction). Equally important, MG1 and MG2 provide thinking strategies for critical reading and writing.

Critical Learning

- MG1 mind grammar: the use of the pattern objective-process for subject matter understanding and critical reading and writing
- MG2 mind grammar: the use of the pattern objective-process-consequences for subject matter comprehension and critical reading and writing

Critical Instruction

The use of MG1 and MG2 mind grammar to explain subject matter while concurrently developing critical thinking, reading, and writing abilities in all students

2. Argumentation strategies

Strategies for identifying and discussing positions and viewpoints on issues, themes, propositions, hypotheses

3. Problem-solving strategies

Strategies for situations that require resolution

Critical Thinking to Understand, Comprehend, and Explain

To explain subject matter critically, teacher–educators, teacher-candidates, school and college faculty, and all of the instructional community[13] must first learn to understand and comprehend subject matter critically.

Instructionally, critical thinking for understanding, comprehension, and explanation is the explicit, reliable, and systematic connection and integration of the ideas and facts associated with the intent, processes, and consequences of a given subject matter topic.

Developing understanding and comprehension of subject matter in students is the essence of professional instructional practice. Therefore, this book emphasizes the use of mind grammar for critical understanding, comprehension, and explanation.

COGERACY

Literacy is the ability to read and write. Numeracy is the ability to calculate. However, there is a need for a general term that addresses the ability to think.

Cogeracy is the ability to think recollectively, logically, critically, and creatively. These represent the four categories of thinking.

Text Box 1.2 summarizes the four categories of thinking.[14]

Text Box 1.2

COGERACY: THE MIND'S PALETTE
THE FOUR CATEGORIES OF THINKING

I. Recall Thinking
To store and recall information

II. Logical (Serial) Thinking
To list persons, places, things, or ideas in some orderly sequence where the concern is the internal serial logic of the list itself and not the meaning, function, or purpose served by the subject matter of the list

III. The Three Modes of Critical Thinking
Strategies for (1) understanding, comprehending, and explaining subject matter; (2) argumentation; and (3) problem solving

IV. Creative Thinking
To discover something new; to be imaginative

CRITICAL LEARNING AND CRITICAL INSTRUCTION

All of the foregoing terms and related ideas provide the basis for critical learning and critical instruction.

Critical Learning

Critical learning is achieving understanding and comprehension[15] of subject matter through use of explicit critical thinking strategies. The thinking strategies are founded on mind grammar, which provides the basis for critical reading and writing. Critical learning is the core of critical instruction.

Critical Instruction

Critical instruction practice is the explicit and critical explanation of how to connect and integrate the objectives, processes, and consequences within subject matter in ways that concurrently develop critical thinking, reading, and writing abilities in all students.

CONSEQUENCES OF MIND GRAMMAR–BASED ASSIGNMENTS

Subject matter universals and mind grammar provide all teachers with rigorous instructional strategies, techniques, and methods. They apply, explicitly and formally, natural thought patterns to all their classroom, homework, and project assignments.

Critical instruction applies our natural mental ability to all subject matter, disciplines, students, and classrooms. Critical instruction allows teaching in ways that all students are innately and, therefore, mentally ready to learn. The result is that we no longer have to teach against the grain of human thought. Students can learn critically in ways that reflect their natural disposition to think critically. Here are the principal positive and neutral consequences of critical instruction and learning.

Positive Consequences of Critical Instruction Practice

Students at All Levels in All Disciplines

All learners, including general students, special education students, English language learners, and disadvantaged students, can now

- have their innate ability to think critically nurtured, developed, and applied;
- achieve understanding and comprehension of new and revisited subject matter in the context of learning to think, read/listen, and write/speak and observe critically;
- develop independent critical learn-to-learn abilities they can carry from class to class, from school to college, and from school or college to the workplace and life;
- engage in critical self-instruction; and

- deal critically with the clouds of information and misinformation they see, read, and hear as presented in all media forms.

The Immediate Instructional Community

In practice, all faculty members in all disciplines and at all grade levels will be set free from the self-defeating impact of serialism strategy on their profession, their practice, and their students. They can now

- promote understanding and comprehension of subject matter while explicitly and concurrently showing students how to think, read, and write critically;
- engage a subject matter topic critically the first time it is discussed in class;
- differentiate instruction using the staged and critical reasoning patterns provided by MG1 and MG2;
- operate learner-centered classrooms where students and teachers transparently and explicitly share critical reasoning patterns; and
- become the true professional leaders of how to transmit subject matter knowledge critically from generation to generation in a learner-centered and shared critically cognitive environment.

The student outcomes of instructional efforts will be substantially more tangible, respected, and universally prized.

Citizens in a Democratic Society

There has always been information presented in ways that are false, in error, distorted, slanted, or confusing. However, the digital age has multiplied greatly the distribution of such information. In a democratic society, the ability to comprehend—to process critically what we see, hear, and read—has never been more important. Mind grammar provides the means for such processing. There are also positive consequences for parents; teacher education programs; writers of standards; organizations that request, submit, and evaluate proposals; textbook/software authors and publishers; and education theorists and researchers. For a discussion, see Maiorana (2016a, Chapter 7).

Neutral Consequences of Critical Instruction Practice

Occasionally, consequences can be neutral. For example, a consequence may require more time, which can be considered negative. However, the additional time may result in a better outcome, which is positive. When such balancing consequences occur, they are considered neutral consequences. Mind grammar is a case in point. It takes time—but surprisingly little time—for both teachers and students to grasp mind grammar strategy. For more on this topic, see Question and Answer 15 in Chapter 2.

In addition, it takes commitment to leave the comfort of the familiar. Intellectual and leadership courage is needed to recognize and act on the irrationality of continuing to rely on the centuries-long, weak, and self-defeating practices of serialism-based learning and instruction. The reward, as described above under positive consequences, is a much more powerful way to teach and learn—one that leads all students to critical comprehension and critical thinking, reading, and writing.

SUMMARY

When it comes to instruction, teachers have a unique responsibility. They must show students not only what they know but also how they know it. Furthermore, it is not enough for teachers to merely model critical thinking, reading, and writing. Students will learn critically only if their teachers explicitly practice critical instruction.

The practice of critical instruction provides the means for teachers to share intellectually the inherent critical nature of subject matter. They can reveal this critical nature explicitly through use of the critical reasoning strategies afforded by mind grammar instructional strategy. This is how teachers can reach a prized goal: showing students through their critically conceived, designed, and applied classroom assignments not only what they know but also how they know it.

QUESTIONS

1. Identify three consequences of a professional language of instruction.
2. What is subject matter and where does it come from?
3. What is the meaning of the term *subject matter universals*?
4. What is mind grammar?
5. How do istrategy, itechnique, and imethod differ?
6. What is serialism and serialism-based instruction?
7. How do the terms *understand* and *comprehend* differ? What does it mean to explain something?
8. Provide an example of describing subject matter versus explaining subject matter.
9. What are the four categories of thinking?
10. Identify the three modes of critical thinking and describe how they differ.

NOTES

1. There are three books that address the need and foundation for and application of a core body of professional knowledge. They are (a) *Fixing Instruction: Resolving Major Issues with a Core Body of Knowledge for Critical Instruction* (Maiorana, 2016a), (b) *Preparation* for *Critical Instruction: How to Explain Subject Matter While Teaching All Learners to Think, Read, and Write Critically* (Maiorana, 2016b), and (c) this book, *Teach Like the Mind Learns: Instruct So Students Learn to Think, Read, and Write Critically*. The need of the profession for a core body of knowledge for instructing critically is introduced in *Fixing Instruction*. How to learn critically, as a basis for instructing critically, is developed explicitly in *Preparation for Critical Instruction*. You should have access to both these works. This will place you in the best position to design and use the critically conceived classroom assignments illustrated in this book.

2. This book is part of the same conception concerning the origination, development, and use of ideas and practices for critical instruction and learning. This makes the three books part of the same writing project. This means that content in *Fixing Instruction* and *Preparation for Critical Instruction* is used and adapted in this work. For example, material from Chapter 1 in *Fixing Instruction* and from Chapter 1 in *Preparation for Critical Instruction* is used in this chapter. Some material from Chapters 2, 3, and 7 in *Fixing Instruction* and from Chapters 2 through 10 in *Preparation for Critical Instruction* is also used and adapted in this work. In addition, for purposes of context, continuity, and emphasis, material appearing in one chapter in this book is repeated in another.

3. See Chapter 1 in *Fixing Instruction*, The Profession Lacks a Language of Instruction (Issue 1). The chapter contains an in-depth study that reveals that despite hundreds of years of practice the teaching profession does not have a coherent and common understanding of the key terms *strategy*, *technique*, and *method.*

4. New subject matter refers to curriculum content that is new to the kindergarten through graduate learner. Revisited subject matter refers to previously discussed content that the learner has not grasped or reviewing content for purposes of reinforcement or test preparation.

5. The terms think(ing), read(ing), and writ(ing) should be taken to apply to thinking, reading, listening, writing, speaking, and observing.

6. When the recitation technique is paired with an instructional strategy it is called the lecture method.

7. For more on the nature of subject matter, see the heading Subject Matter Speaks in *Preparation for Critical Instruction*, page 41.

8. Your author originated the concepts of subject matter universals and mind grammar and their application to engaging new and revisited subject matter.

9. See discussion of serialism earlier in this chapter under Examples of Istrategies.

10. For more on the limitations of graphic organizers as a means to understand, comprehend, and explain subject matter critically, see *Fixing Instruction*, pages 27 and 28.

11. The term *problem solving* is used broadly here to refer to situations requiring or desiring resolution. This includes scientific observation and investigation.

12. See *Fixing Instruction* for an in-depth and complete explanation of this issue.

13. There are three parts to the instructional community: immediate, related, and extended. The *immediate instructional community* includes teacher–educators, teacher-candidates, school and college faculty, counselors, teacher aides, professional developers, parents who homeschool, curriculum and instruction designers, principals, and assistant principals. The *related community* includes education school deans, school and college faculty deans, program directors, parents, tutors, school boards, parent–teacher associations, researchers and writers, and textbook authors and publishers in all media. It includes organizations that establish teacher certification criteria and that engage in certification processes; organizations that write, issue, adopt, and support standards; and unions and professional associations and organizations. The *extended community* includes district and state superintendents, chancellors, and boards of regents; local, state, and federal congressional committees, lawmakers, and policymakers; local, state, and federal departments of education; and public and private grant-funding organizations that have interest in and support education.

14. For a complete discussion of cogeracy, see Chapter 3, Thinking: The First Language Art, in *Preparation for Critical Instruction.*

15. See prior discussion in this chapter for the difference between critical understanding and critical comprehension. For a grounding in how to learn critically, see Chapters 2 through 9 in *Preparation for Critical Instruction.*

BIBLIOGRAPHY

Maiorana, V. P. (2016a). *Fixing instruction: Resolving major issues with a core body of knowledge for critical instruction.* Lanham, MD: Rowman & Littlefield.

Maiorana, V. P. (2016b). *Preparation for critical instruction: How to explain subject matter while teaching all learners to think, read, and write critically.* Lanham, MD: Rowman & Littlefield.

Merriam-Webster's collegiate dictionary (11th ed.). (2007). Springfield, MA: Merriam-Webster.

Vygotsky, L. S. (1976). Problems of method. In M. Cole, V. John-Steiner, A. Scribner, & E. Souberman (Eds.), *Mind in society: The development of higher psychological processes* (pp. 58–75). Cambridge, MA: Harvard University Press.

Chapter Two

The Mind Grammar Instructional Set

Subject Matter Objective: The end-in-view of a mind grammar instructional set is to have students achieve understanding and comprehension of new and revisited subject matter topics through pairing mind grammar instructional strategies with instructional techniques that develop critical thinking, reading, listening, writing, speaking, and observing abilities in all students.

The materials in this book address the practice of *critical* instruction based on mind grammar instructional strategy. They illustrate how to understand and comprehend new and revisited subject matter. Explanations are critical and explicit. The critical reasoning strategies used are transparent. This means they are to be shared clearly and formally with students.

Explanations proceed in ways that concurrently develop critical thinking, reading, and writing abilities in all students. Explanations are based on the design of classroom assignments. Such assignments are the means by which one practices critical instruction.

It is expected that the reader has already been prepared to practice critical instruction. This may have been achieved through a teacher preparation program or professional development program or through access to the work *Preparation for Critical Instruction: How to Explain Subject Matter While Teaching All Learners to Think, Read, and Write Critically* (Maiorana, 2016b). However, there are several instructional sets in Chapters 4 through 7 that introduce mind grammar–based critical learning. See the headings Introducing Students to Critical Learning and Questions and Answers Regarding Critical Instruction later on in this chapter.

THE ESSENCE OF CLASSROOM PRACTICE

As a teacher-candidate, inservice teacher, instructional developer, or professional developer practicing at the primary or secondary level, you likely prepare lesson plans. If you teach at the postsecondary or graduate level; in adult, continuing, or workplace education; or are a postsecondary professional developer, your preparation may take a different form. In any event, classroom assignments that engage students with subject matter are needed.

Classroom assignments are an expression of a teacher's professional instructional practice. They are the essence of a lesson plan[1] and lesson plan activity. Therefore, this chapter concerns the practice of critical instruction as realized through the design of mind grammar–based classroom assignments.

WHAT IS A MIND GRAMMAR INSTRUCTIONAL SET?

Description

An instructional set is a collection of classroom assignments that address a specific subject matter topic. The assignments use instructional techniques, with mind grammar as the instructional strategy. There are two mind grammar strategies for explaining subject matter. MG1 achieves understanding. MG2 achieves comprehension.[2,3] The mind grammar strategies provide students with the ability to engage new or revisited subject matter while concurrently leading them to think, read, and write critically.

Teacher Resources

To maintain professionalism, when you develop an instructional set, the resources you use to design the assignments should appear at the end of each set. Resources can include a subject matter display, which provides a critical view of a given topic; critically written narratives; other materials; references; and notes on how to use the assignments in the classroom.

When you use the set again at a later date or it is used by a colleague, the resources will be at hand. This is especially important for those resources that are used with or handed out to students. The instructional sets in Chapters 4 through 7 illustrate the foregoing.

HOW TO DEVELOP AND USE A MIND GRAMMAR INSTRUCTIONAL SET

The procedure to develop and use a mind grammar instructional set is shown in Text Box 2.1.[4]

Text Box 2.1

PROCEDURE TO DEVELOP AND USE AN INSTRUCTIONAL SET

1. Select a specific subject matter topic.
2. Select a critical reasoning strategy (MG1 and/or MG2) to explain the topic.
3. Develop a subject matter display.
4. Design classroom assignments.
5. Assemble, use, assess, and revise the instructional set.

Here is a discussion of each item in Text Box 2.1.

SELECT A SPECIFIC SUBJECT MATTER TOPIC

Select a Topic

The use of mind grammar starts with identifying a specific subject matter topic. The topic may be broad (e.g., the Milky Way Galaxy) or relatively narrow (e.g., the Earth's moon). The topic you select must

- be specific,
- not include another topic, and
- be clearly stated in context.

For example, consider this topic: "The Galaxy and the Moon." This is a weak topic description because it does not address a specific galaxy or a specific moon, two topics are addressed, and there is no context.

Rewriting the topic as "The Milky Way Galaxy and the Earth's Moon" is an improvement, but we are still left with two main topics to explain. The display you develop (e.g., a four-stage MG2 display) must then include two objectives, two sets of activities, two sets of consequences, and two sets of resources. To minimize display confusion and complexity, it is better to treat each topic in its own display. In addition, there is still no context. To provide a specific, single, and contextual topic a better description would be "The Milky Way Galaxy and Its Relationship to the Earth's Moon."

Focusing on the Earth's moon, here are some examples of topics. They are specific, address one main topic (the Earth's moon), and are in context: The Impact of the Earth's Moon on the Earth's Ocean Tides, The Romantic Aspects of the Earth's Moon, and How the United States Landed Men on the Earth's Moon.

Use the Topic in the Title of Your Display

In making clear the subject matter topic, you accomplish two things. First, you clarify for yourself and your students exactly what you are to teach and what your students are to learn. Second, the topic you identify also serves as the title for your subject matter display, for example, A Subject Matter Display of How the United States Landed Men on the Earth's Moon.

SELECT A CRITICAL REASONING STRATEGY (MG1 OR MG2) TO EXPLAIN THE TOPIC

Teaching is a profession built on thinking directed at subject matter. The absence of a critical reasoning strategy leads one to describe subject matter serially rather than explain it critically. The result is rote learning and the defeat of your students' critical skills development.[5]

To instruct students in subject matter through critical thinking, reading, and writing, one must use a formal, explicit, and shared critical reasoning strategy. That strategy must provide the reasoning basis to not only think critically of subject matter but to read and write of it as well. Mind grammar is such a strategy.

Mind grammar[6] is the innate, systematic, and patterned way that the human mind develops and encounters the world and all its subject matter. It is a natural system of thinking that provides the basis for critical instruction and critical learning.

Innate mind grammar provides the means to critically understand, comprehend, and explain subject matter. Mind grammar reasoning patterns reveal, connect, and integrate the objective, processes, and consequences universally present within all subject matter.

Two mind grammar reasoning patterns are used and are referred to as MG1 and MG2. They provide the foundation to critically explain subject matter. They provide as well the reasoning basis for critical reading and writing.

DEVELOP A SUBJECT MATTER DISPLAY

A subject matter display allows one to connect and integrate critically the universal attributes associated with a given subject topic. The very acts of thinking of and writing out these related thoughts in a "word picture" provide the means of gaining one's self-understanding and comprehension of a topic.

With respect to professional instructional practice, a complete display is the basis for explaining a topic critically. There are two types of mind grammar displays.

Types of Subject Matter Displays

Subject matter displays are based on either MG1 or MG2.

Use MG1 to Achieve Understanding

- Two-stage MG1 display: includes display title, subject matter objective, and activities.
- Three-stage MG1 display: includes display title, subject matter objective, activities, and resources.

Use MG2 to Achieve Comprehension

- Three-stage MG2 display: includes display title, subject matter objective, activities, and consequences.
- Four-stage MG2 display: includes display title, subject matter objective, activities, consequences, and resources.

Examples of subject matter displays appear in Chapter 3. For a full discussion of the nature, development, and assessment of subject matter displays, see Chapter 5,

Understand Critically with Mind Grammar One, and Chapter 6, Comprehend Critically with Mind Grammar Two, both in *Preparation for Critical Instruction: How to Explain Subject Mătter While Teaching All Learners to Think, Read, and Write Critically* (Maiorana, 2016b).

Decide Which Display Type to Use

Decide whether you will use a two- or three-stage MG1 display, or a three- or four-stage MG2 display. Base your decision on (a) the topic at hand and its degree of difficulty—with a difficult topic, start with an MG1 display and then transition to an MG2 display; (b) the grade level and background of your students (e.g., regular, special, ELL, disadvantaged, or blended); (c) the importance of the topic; (d) how much time you wish to devote to the topic; and (e) how familiar your students are with mind grammar strategy.

Subject matter displays covering a variety of topics are available from several sources. These include displays developed by yourself, colleagues, or other sources, such as this textbook. Keep in mind that instructional sets can be developed even if you do not have a subject matter display for the topic at hand. There is a great advantage of teaching and sharing a critical reasoning strategy with your students. You can call on their developing capabilities to think, read, and write critically to self-direct their learning. The ability of students to self-direct their learning provides you with great classroom flexibility in assisting those students who may need help.

At some point, students will become reasonably proficient in developing subject matter displays. This point can occur after three to four weeks of exposure to mind grammar strategy two to three times a week. Here is an example of an itechnique you can use that does not require the formal development of an instructional asset. When reasonably proficient with mind grammar, ask students to listen and take notes as you deliver a short lecture on a new or revisited topic. Then have the students translate their notes into a subject matter display.

Another itechnique is to ask students to read about a new or revisited topic in a textbook, on a web page, or in other material. Then have them reconstruct critically what they have read into a subject matter display.

The Subject Matter Narrative

A subject matter narrative is your written expression of a corresponding subject matter display.[7] You prepare a narrative when you are going to employ an itechnique that is based on the narrative.

The discussion may follow the order of the display. However, you may alter the order of discussion to suit personal or instructional preferences. The discussion can include material not in the display. Let your personality show through. Be conversational. Try to tell a story in the context of a real-life or career/workplace situation. Avoid long sentences. Be sure to use quotation marks when appropriate. Be sure to cite your research sources. When they write their own narratives, encourage your students to follow these approaches as well. Remember that your students are likely to use the narratives you distribute as examples of good writing.

Summary of Subject Matter Display Guidelines

Text Box 2.2 contains guidelines for developing a subject matter display.

Text Box 2.2

HOW TO DEVELOP A SUBJECT MATTER DISPLAY

1. Identify a single and specific subject matter topic. Use the topic in the title of your subject matter display.

2. Your display must contain only one subject matter objective. Write the subject matter objective in the form of a complete sentence. Use any one of the following forms you think is appropriate for the topic at hand: end-in-view *or* effect *or* importance *or* meaning *or* purpose *or* function or another similar term you select. Here are some examples:

The end-in-view of [name of topic] *is to* _________.
The meaning of [name of topic] *is* _________.
The effect of [name of topic] *is* _________.

For more on how to develop a single specific topic and its associated subject matter objective, see Chapter 5 in *Preparation for Critical Instruction.*

A subject matter objective bears no relation to and is independent of the objectives held by teachers, students, and authors. Statements such as "The student shall understand [name of topic]" are not valid statements of subject matter objectives. They do not belong in a subject matter display because such behavioral objectives address the student and not the subject matter topic. Such statements are not valid expressions of the topic's end-in-view, effect, importance, meaning, purpose, or function.

A subject matter objective must always advance the explanation and not simply be a restatement of the title. In addition, a subject matter objective must not include a consequence.

3. Decide whether to use an MG1 or MG2 display. For a discussion of display types, see *Preparation for Critical Instruction*, Chapters 5 and 6.

4. The activities must address the subject matter directly, in other words, describe or develop the activities needed to achieve the subject matter objective.

All the activities must be listed in logical order. To promote clarity, favor the use of short statements or phrases.

To reduce complexity, try to keep the list of activities to ten or fewer. If you have a long list of activities (i.e., more than ten), consider breaking the activities into two or more groups, each with its own heading (e.g., see Figure 4.6).

Classroom assignments do not belong under activities because such assignments address activities for students, not subject matter.

5. A consequence is what can happen if a subject matter objective is achieved or not achieved, realized or not realized. Consequences can be positive or negative and short term or long term. For a discussion of how to develop consequences, see Chapter 6 in *Preparation for Critical Instruction.*

6. The resources must address the subject matter directly, in other words, identify the resources that are explicit and implicit in the subject matter activities. The words "student," "study," "textbook," "teacher," and "school" *do not belong as resources* because they are not needed to achieve the end-in-view, effect, importance, meaning, purpose, or function *of the subject matter topic.* Group the resources by persons, places, things, and ideas.

7. Include a vocabulary box for terms that are new to you and are likely to be new to your students. Include common terms used in a specialized way.

8. Keep your subject matter displays clear and concise.

Remember, your subject matter display must be truly critical. To be so, it must apply mind grammar properly. Otherwise, your display-based classroom assignments will not induce critical thinking, reading, and writing in your students. See Chapters 4 through 7 for many examples of subject matter displays.

DESIGN CLASSROOM ASSIGNMENTS

Designing classroom assignments involves considering the type of assignment, the number of assignments to include in an instructional set, the time needed to complete an assignment, and the itechniques to use in an assignment.

Types of Classroom Assignments

Assignments can ask students to engage in a variety of active and critical learning activities. Assignments can ask students to reason, read, write, listen, speak, observe, and apply. Note that all assignments, of necessity, also involve reasoning.

The essential nature of an assignment depends on your instructional intent. For example, assume your intent is to have students write a summary of reading material you provide. Such an assignment will require students to read and think critically. However, it would be considered a writing assignment because that is your instructional intent.

A Reasoning Assignment

A reasoning assignment asks students to think of new or revisited subject matter critically to achieve understanding and comprehension. For a full discussion on thinking critically of subject matter, see Chapter 5, Critical Understanding with Mind Grammar One, and Chapter 6, Critical Comprehension with Mind Grammar Two, both in *Preparation for Critical Instruction.*

A Reading Assignment

A reading assignment asks students to read critically using MG1 or MG2. The material to be read can be conventional textbooks, newspaper articles, magazine articles, computer-based educational materials, content and social websites, and other sources. For a full discussion on reading critically, see Chapter 7, Read for Critical Comprehension, in *Preparation for Critical Instruction.*

A Listening Assignment

A listening assignment asks students to take notes and then reconstruct them critically. Preparing for such an assignment is similar to reading critically. See A Reading Assignment, above.

A Writing Assignment

A writing assignment asks students to compose a series of sentences and paragraphs that explain a given topic critically. A subject matter display is used as a writing framework. See the discussion above under The Subject Matter Narrative. For a full discussion of writing for critical explanation, see Chapter 8, Write for Critical Explanation, in *Preparation for Critical Instruction.*

A Speaking Assignment

A speaking assignment asks students to deliver a critically composed talk. Preparing for such an assignment is similar to writing critically. See A Writing Assignment above.

An Observing Assignment

An observing assignment asks students to view something and then report on it (through writing or speaking) critically. For example, the "something" can take the form of observing a street scene, an animal, a plant, bacteria (via a microscope), a photograph, or an oil painting.

An Application Assignment

An application assignment asks students to apply what they now understand and comprehend. For example, say an instructional set addresses the First Amendment to the US Constitution. An application assignment would ask students to apply what they learned about critically engaging the First Amendment to another amendment.

A Homework Assignment

A homework assignment simply asks students, for a given topic, to engage at home in one or more of the preceding assignments.

The Number of Assignments in an Instructional Set

The number of assignments to include in an instructional set is up to you. As with the subject matter display, base your decision on (a) the topic at hand and its degree of difficulty, (b) the grade level and background of your students, (c) the importance of the topic, (d) how much time you wish to devote to the topic, and (e) how familiar your students are with mind grammar strategy.

Ideally, and if time were unlimited, all class meetings would include assignments that ask students to reason, read, write, listen, speak, observe, and apply. But this is not realistic. However, it is realistic to include such assignments during one or more weeks of instruction.

Assignment Duration

Any given assignment can last five, ten, or twenty minutes; a whole period; or more. Clearly, the more important you consider the topic, the more assignments you will develop and the more time will be required to complete such assignments.

Writing an Assignment

Favor short sentences of fifteen or fewer words. Assignments should be self-explanatory. They should allow students to work in a self-directed manner.

When writing an assignment, talk directly to the student. Here is an example of what not to do. It is followed by an example of what to do.

- [What Not to Do] *Assignment 1—Read the First Amendment for Critical Comprehension:* Here is the First Amendment to the Constitution of the United States. The student shall read the amendment using the MG2 critical reading procedure. The student shall work by herself or himself.
- [What to Do] *Assignment 1—Read the First Amendment for Critical Comprehension:* Here is the First Amendment to the Constitution of the United States. Read it using the MG2 critical reading procedure. Work by yourself.

Selecting Which Itechnique(s) to Use in an Assignment

A great variety of instructional techniques are available and they are described in Chapter 3. In general, select itechniques based on the background of your students, the difficulty level of the subject matter of the topic, the importance of the topic, and the class time you wish to devote to the topic.

For difficult topics, special education students, and blended classes you can use a developmental approach. In other words, avoid engaging students with all the mind grammar elements in a subject matter display in one assignment. Instead, engage the elements over two or more assignments.

You are by no means tied to using the itechniques described in Chapter 3. Your experience with the nature and use of mind grammar will grow. This in turn will allow you to create or adapt itechniques that work especially well with the nature of the students in your class and the subject matter you teach.

You will find it most gratifying when you create your own itechniques or develop variations on existing ones.

ASSEMBLE, USE, ASSESS, AND REVISE THE INSTRUCTIONAL SET

Assemble the Instructional Set

Assembling an instructional set allows you to assess its state of completeness, provide for its future reference and use, prepare it for reproduction and distribution (hard copy or digital), and share easily your design work with colleagues.

In addition to classroom assignments, an instructional set can include a section that addresses teacher resources. Teacher resources include fully developed subject matter displays, narratives, suggestions on how to use the assignments in class, references used in designing the set, identification of itechniques that you have self-developed or adapted, exams that assess the degree of student learning, and recommendations on how to further develop the set.

Examples of assembled instructional sets are shown in Chapters 3 through 7.

Use the Instructional Set

Distribute assignments in class (via hard copy, digital copy, screen projection, board description, or verbally). It is good practice to first review the assignment with students to answer any questions that may arise.

Circulate among the students as they work on the assignments. Offer encouragement to those who are proceeding correctly. Offer help and encouragement to those who may be having difficulty. Consider pairing students who know how to proceed with others who may need help. If a good portion of the class seems to be having trouble, ask for their attention and clarify the assignment.

Assess the Instructional Set

To assess an instructional set means to evaluate how well the assignments worked out in class. This includes taking notes on observations that you make as well as remarks made by students. Such notes can then be used to help prepare an assessment report.

There are a number of assessment factors to consider, and they are shown in Table 2.1. It is best to complete the table as soon as practicable after a class meeting.

Table 2.1. Assignment Assessment Factors

Factors to Consider When Assessing the Use of Assignments Within an Instructional Set	**Notes** *(Use this column to answer the questions posed in column 1.)*
1. Did most students complete the assignments satisfactorily?	
2. What observations, by assignment number, did you make regarding improving the assignments?	
3. What remarks, by assignment number, did students make as they worked on the assignments?	
4. Were assignments properly sequenced?	
5. Should an assignment be made into two or more assignments? Which ones?	
6. Should some assignments be combined? If so, which ones?	
7. Should certain assignments be deleted? If so, which ones?	
8. Was enough time budgeted to complete the assignments? Which assignments needed more time to complete?	

Revise the Instructional Set

To revise an instructional set means to correct errors, improve clarity, and rewrite the directions within the assignments as needed. If possible, record found errors in real time on your copy of the set. This will help ensure the set is updated as necessary.

Students may find errors or ambiguity in a subject matter display, a narrative, or assignment instructions. They may see a better way of stating a subject matter objective. They may provide better sequencing of activities. They may see consequences from a unique perspective. If a comment is not valid, do not just dismiss it. Explain why, and if possible, try to find a way to make the comment fit within the discussion. You should, of course, accept valid comments with praise. You should also rejoice. It shows that your efforts to lead students to think, read, and write critically are succeeding.

INTRODUCING STUDENTS TO CRITICAL LEARNING

Informally

In the informal approach, and regardless of grade level and discipline, you just start to talk critically for understanding (MG1). You use a neutral topic (anything you select), a new topic, or revisit a topic previously discussed. After several sessions, you can start to summarize class discussions critically. You can do this by introducing students to a "word picture" in the form of a two-stage or three-stage MG1 subject matter display. You can then ask students to summarize the class discussion by writing a narrative based on the MG1 display. You then expand your discussions to address comprehension (MG2).

Formally

Here is a way to start the formal introduction to mind grammar. You can say: "All humans are born with the innate ability to think critically. We use this gift in an informal way every day. We can apply that innate critical ability in a formal way to the topics we study in this course. Called mind grammar, it involves identifying a subject matter topic's objective, associated activities, and consequences. This pattern represents a formal critical reasoning strategy. I would now like to share that reasoning strategy with you in a formal and explicit way."[8]

The following instructional sets are examples of how to formally introduce students to critical learning: in Chapter 4, Let's Explore the Story of Jack and Jill, Let's Explore Further the Story of Jack and Jill, Introduction to Critical Learning, and Introduction to Critical Learning for English Language Learners; in Chapter 5, A Wild Style of Painting, Music, and The Battle of Gettysburg; in Chapter 6, The Circle, Geography, and Electrically Charged Clouds; and in Chapter 7, An Economic System.

QUESTIONS AND ANSWERS REGARDING CRITICAL INSTRUCTION PRACTICE

1. *Why can't teacher–educators, school and college faculty, and professional developers continue to instruct the way they always have?*

They can, but they will continue to unwittingly undermine their own best efforts. Teaching is a profession built on thinking directed at subject matter. Yet as a profession, teaching is practiced without a critically cognitive foundation in either thinking or subject matter. Since thinking is the first language art, this means there is no cognitive foundation for reading or writing critically. Without a core body of knowledge for critical instruction, teachers will continue self-defeating conventional practice.

Conventional practice is based on using self-defeating serialism as an instructional strategy. Serialism denies the mind's innate ability to think critically using our innate grammar of mind. This is so because serialism does not represent a critical reasoning strategy for connecting and integrating facts and ideas. The result is rote learning.

When engaging new or revisited subject matter, serialism provides no cognitive basis for the development of critical thinking, reading, listening, writing, speaking, and observing abilities in students. To achieve a full appreciation of the serialism issue and to see its negative consequences for the profession and students at all levels, see *Fixing Instruction: Resolving Major Issues with a Core Body of Knowledge for Critical Instruction* (Maiorana, 2016a).

2. *So serialism-induced rote learning is of limited value?*

Let's start by establishing what is commonly meant by rote learning. According to *Merriam-Webster's Collegiate Dictionary* (2007, p. 1084), rote learning is "the use of memory usually with little intelligence . . . unthinking routine or repetition . . . a joyless sense of order [i.e., serialism]."

All learning is of value. However, our aim as teacher–educators, teacher-candidates, and school and college faculty is to lead *all* students at *all* levels to think, read, and write critically. Rote learning is a weak, unthinking, and joyless intellectual dead end. However, the issue is not that rote learning itself is of limited value.

Here is the issue. The use of rote-inducing serialism-based instruction—beginning in the early grades and continuing on through college—denies teachers the ability to lead students to use their innate grammar of mind to think critically. This in turn defeats the ability to read and write critically when engaging new and revisited subject matter.

Therefore, the main drawback of rote learning is that it provides no reasoning foundation for reasoning critically. This means as well that rote learning provides no reasoning foundation for reading and writing critically. Consequences for faculty include frustration and high rates of early departure from the profession and for students, poor academic achievement and high dropout rates in schools and colleges.

To think, read, and write critically when engaging new and revisited subject matter, one needs a critical reasoning strategy. Humans have the gift of an innate grammar of mind. That gift provides the basis for a formal critical reasoning strategy when engaging subject matter. That strategy is called mind grammar. The power of mind grammar strategy is that it allows both teachers and students at all levels to formally (a) connect and integrate critically facts and ideas already in their possession into a subject matter display (or its equivalent), (b) connect and integrate into a display facts and ideas encountered when reading *new or revisited subject matter*, and (c) use a display as an outline to write critically. See *Preparation for Critical Instruction: How to Explain Subject Matter While Teaching All Learners to Think, Read, and Write Critically* (Maiorana, 2016b).

3. *Must I develop a critical view (a subject matter display) for every topic I teach?*

If a topic is new to you, then for purposes of your preparation to practice critical instruction, you will want to comprehend it critically. So preparing a subject matter display or an equivalent would be in order.

With practice and help from you, students learn to more fully develop their innate mind grammar ability. They are able to take on more and more responsibility for their own critical learning. They become your active learning partner. With practice, your students will become competent in thinking, reading, and writing critically.

At that point, you can ask them to develop a subject matter display based on reading or listening to materials that address course subject matter. Under such conditions, it is not necessary for you to develop a display for the assigned material. Your focus becomes evaluating your students' MG1 and MG2 displays to see if they are valid.

The subject matter display is simply an instrument for connecting and integrating subject matter universals so they may be grasped in a critically assembled manner. Your instructional creativity will lead you to develop other ways to represent the elements that appear in a subject matter display.

4. *How do I know whether to use an MG1 or MG2 subject matter display?*

Which one to use depends on the grade level of your class, the nature of your students (disadvantaged, ELL, regular, special, or blended), the difficulty level of the subject matter topic, the importance of the topic, and the class time you wish to devote to the topic.

In a typical course, some topics are considered more important than others. For those topics, you will want a deeper level of engagement. Use a three- or four-stage MG2 subject matter display. For difficult topics, start at the MG1 level and then move on to an MG2 discussion. For other topics, you can limit the discussion to two- or three-stage MG1 displays.

5. *Can I bypass a subject matter display and go straight to writing an MG1 or MG2 narrative and then use the narrative as a basis for designing an instructional set?*

Yes. At some point you will internalize formally and use fluidly the MG1 and MG2 strategies. You will be able to visualize a subject matter display and write accordingly.

6. *Can mind grammar be used in special education classes?*

Yes. Do not assume that special education students cannot be engaged critically with mind grammar. They can, because like all students, it is part of their nature.

Start with logical thinking exercises. Base these on the discussion of logical thinking in Chapter 3, Thinking: The First Language Art, in *Preparation for Critical Instruction.* Then transition to modest two-stage MG1 displays. Then move to three-stage MG1 displays and then on to MG2.

When moving to MG2, consider starting with a two-stage MG2 display that contains only a subject matter objective and consequences. Then add activities as the bridge between the two to arrive at a three-stage MG2 display. Based on your sense of the class, you can then move to a four-stage MG2 display.

7. *How do I engage in differentiation in my blended classes when using critical instruction?*

Differentiation is using different learning approaches with different students within a class. For example, with critical instruction, different itechniques can be used within a class. Students can work on some version of an MG1 or MG2 display. Some students develop a two-stage MG1 display and the others a three-stage MG1 display.

Differentiation can also be achieved by pairing or grouping students with a good knowledge of mind grammar with those still learning the mind grammar strategies. The process can start by having students develop an MG1 display. They can then move on to an MG2 in a similar manner. Some of the first ten itechniques described in Chapter 3 lend themselves to differentiation, as do others described in the chapter.

8. *How do I use mind grammar with English language learners?*

English language learners have a twofold challenge. At the same time, they must learn a new language and deal with meaning-defeating and language arts–defeating serialism.

All humans share the same mind grammar thought structure of intent-process-consequences. All languages share the same subject-verb-direct object structure of the sentence. Like the sentence, mind grammar is the innate, systematic, and patterned way the human mind repeatedly encounters and reflects on the world. These ideas, as a basis of learning both a new language and the subject matter at hand, makes moving between languages natural and predictable. For examples of how this is done, refer to the ELL-based instructional sets in Chapter 4. Note that all the itechniques described in Chapter 3 can be used with any language.

9. *How does critical instruction address critical reading?*

Reading approaches, such as close reading, are inherently weak because they are based on serialism thinking strategy. Serialism does not represent a critical reading strategy. Therefore, it has no power to represent subject matter text critically. For a discussion of the great limitations and drawbacks of serialism and conventional approaches to reading for comprehension, see Chapter 2, Instructional Practice Is Inherently Weak: The Hidden Story, in *Fixing Instruction*. Without an *explicitly shared* critical reasoning strategy in play, teachers—regardless of discipline—cannot effectively assess the degree of student comprehension of textual material.

To read critically, students must be taught a critical reasoning strategy. Only when they possess such a strategy will they be independent critical readers. Mind grammar represents a reasoning strategy not only for critical thinking but for critical reading and writing as well. Mind grammar is a systematic, reproducible, and transferable way to read for critical comprehension. It provides the ability to connect and integrate ideas critically. Critical reading for understanding is the application of MG1 mind grammar to textual material. Critical reading for comprehension is the application of MG2 mind grammar to textual material.

How students can learn to read critically can be found in Chapter 7, Read for Critical Comprehension, in *Preparation for Critical Instruction.* See instructional sets in Chapters 4 through 7 in this book for application examples of critical reading assignments.

10. *When reading critically, must I mark the text for the elements of mind grammar?*

In a learning situation, the common approach to reading textual material is to mark the material through underlining or highlighting. The thought is, "This sounds important, I'll underline it now and come back to it later." Underlining is serialism. It represents the serial marking of facts and ideas without a reasoning basis for connecting and integrating them critically. See the answer to question 9 above.

If you are just learning to use MG1 and MG2 for reading critically, then it is necessary to mark the text in some way. Rather than just underlining material that seems important, you can develop your own mind grammar–based marking system. For example, if a line of text contains an activity, mark the line in the margin with an "a" or simply make an entry in your notebook. So, yes, when first learning to use mind grammar when reading, you should mark the text. You can use the marking approach given in Figure 4.7 on reading for critical comprehension or develop your own marking system.

Is it important that you comprehend deeply a given subject matter topic? The answer is again yes, although the degree to which you mark text (as opposed to taking notes) is up to you. When reading critically has become second nature to you, there will be little need to mark the text. Instead, you can take notes as you read, writing down key mind grammar elements. You can then use your notes to summarize the text in subject matter display format or in some other format. Remember, if you are using MG2 and the textual material lacks a discussion of consequences, then you will need to develop them yourself.

11. *How does critical instruction address critical writing?*

When given a writing assignment, students are encouraged to use a writing plan. A typical plan includes the preparation of an outline that includes an introduction, body, and conclusion. In the introduction they are to state their topic and thesis. In the body they are instructed to write paragraphs. Each paragraph is to have a topic sentence supported by facts and ideas. In the conclusion, they are to summarize what they discovered or now understand or believe about their topic.

The main weakness with the typical outlining process is that the very things students are asked to do are the very things they have great difficulty with. How, explicitly, do they develop an outline? How do they use the outline to write topic sentences and associated paragraphs? How do they draw conclusions? The standard outlining process is largely ineffective because it does not address these issues. This is shown by state English Language Arts exams that ask students to write an essay. Such exams often provide a topic theme, but they also provide an outline of the issues to address and considerations for the conclusions to be drawn.

In other words, with such mental prompts, the exam writer provides the necessary thinking. The student follows the prescription. When placed in situations where such mental supports are absent, such as in a school or college or on the job, they are essentially lost.

Mind grammar provides students with a critical reasoning strategy that has long been missing from the typical writing plan. Consequently, students have the independent means to engage in the necessary critical thinking that outlining and writing for explanation requires.[9]

12. *Say a subject matter display is developed in class. I then ask my students to write a narrative based on that display. If students use the same subject matter display as an outline for writing, won't all their narratives be similar?*

Initially, yes. Keep in mind that your aim is to teach students how to write critically of your discipline's topics. If they do write similar mind grammar–based narratives, you will have succeeded, and they as well. Initially, this is what you want to happen.

Their narratives will be similar in this way: They will write of a topic's objective, activities, consequences, and resources. In other words, their narratives will be critically organized because you have taught them to explicitly and formally think critically. You will also have taught them to write sentences that cohere in paragraph form. This is a major achievement that can be accomplished only if students base their writing on the use of critical reasoning strategies such as MG1 and MG2.

As students gain confidence in their critical writing abilities, they are free to experiment and apply their creativity. They can write their narratives in any order they see fit and in ways that reflect their individual uniqueness. They can also include related information in the narrative that is not in the display. The only requirement is that the elements of mind grammar be integrated into the discussion.

For more on writing narratives, see the discussion on The Subject Matter Narrative, earlier in this chapter. For an example of how students can progress from writing "similar narratives" to unique ones, see Text Boxes 8.1 through 8.3 in Chapter 8, Write for Critical Explanation, in *Preparation for Critical Instruction*.

13. *How does critical instruction address the idea that teachers must adapt their instructional activities to the different learning styles of students?*

Students do have individual and different sensory and media preferences for *taking in* information. Once information is taken in, different students may have different reactions to that information. They may think of different questions to ask. They may see things that others do not. They may apply the information in uniquely creative ways. Their curiosity may be stimulated in different ways. So, yes, students are very different in the ways just described.

However, do they have different ways of processing the information to arrive at initial understanding once information has entered the mind? No, not when it comes to gaining understanding and comprehension. For a given topic we are all disposed in some way to use our innate mind grammar pattern. That is to say, gaining understanding and then comprehension of subject matter is eventually the result of identifying intent, ordering the activities needed to achieve the intent, and evaluating the consequences that ensue. When it comes to how the mind understands and comprehends, this grammar of mind is shared innately by all.

The mind must eventually process information no matter the form in which it is received. The innate elements of mind grammar are always at work and respond to all forms of information reception.

14. *Don't you have to know some facts and ideas concerning a topic before you can think critically of it?*

When the topic of critical thinking comes up, those engaging in the discussion must first agree on what they mean by critical thinking. There are three modes of critical thinking. Mode 1 concerns understanding, comprehending, and explaining a subject matter topic critically. Mode 2 concerns argumentation. Mode 3 concerns situational resolution (e.g., problem solving). For full discussions of these three modes, see Chapter 3 in *Fixing Instruction* and Chapter 3 in *Preparation for Critical Instruction.*

If you are concerned with thinking critically for understanding, comprehension, and explanation (Mode 1 of critical thinking and the main concern of teachers), knowing facts and ideas in advance is helpful, but not necessary. What *is* necessary is having possession of an explicit critical reasoning strategy (e.g., MG1 or MG2). You can obtain facts and ideas on any given topic *by using the critical reasoning strategy itself as the basis for asking questions of the subject matter.* See the topics Subject Matter Speaks and The Mind Grammar Interview Procedure, on pages 41 and 48, respectively, in *Preparation for Critical Instruction.*

You then take the facts and ideas elicited (whether new to you or not, and no matter how they are gathered or presented), and connect and integrate them critically. That *same* mind grammar reasoning strategy provides the basis for critical reading and writing (see Chapters 7 and 8 in *Preparation for Critical Instruction*).

Based on mind grammar reasoning strategy, the subject matter display is a way to connect and integrate facts and ideas critically (again, whether new to you or not). For more on this, see the Mind Grammar Interview Procedure in Chapter 4 in *Preparation for Critical Instruction.*

If you are interested in modes 2 and 3 of critical thinking (argumentation and problem solving), mere possession of facts and ideas is again of small value. To engage effectively in argumentation or problem solving, you must first critically comprehend, or at least critically understand, the issue being debated or the problem requiring resolution. In other words, you must first engage in mode 1 of critical thinking. You can then go on to mode 2 and/or mode 3.

Accordingly, it is not necessary to first memorize facts and ideas as a prelude to thinking critically. This widely held belief is based on the profession's long-held reliance on serialism-based instruction.[10] This belief puts the cart before the horses. With the advent of mind grammar, the horses are placed before the cart. The leading horse is mode 1 of critical thinking. The two following horses, hitched side by side, are modes 2 and 3. The cart contains the facts and ideas, whether new or revisited.

Without the critical horses you cannot pull the facts and ideas into a state of criticality. You have only crystallized information waiting for someone to come along and warm them up critically. With mind grammar as an instructional strategy, that someone is you, the professional teacher, a teacher who, by practicing critical instruction, can lead students to think, read, and write critically while simultaneously engaging new and revisited subject matter.

15. *How can I cover the required material* and *do the extra work of teaching students to think, read, and write critically?*

This question is related to question 14. It assumes that the teaching of subject matter is *something apart* from simultaneously thinking, reading, and writing about it critically.[11] Again, this idea is tied to the conventional practice of serialism-based instruction (see the heading Examples of Istrategies in Chapter 1 and endnote 13 in this chapter).

Although this is the traditional view, teaching students to think, read, and write critically is no longer a matter of "extra work." With mind grammar, teaching and learning critically is a matter of "right now" and "concurrency." Teaching critically is a chorus, not consecutive solos.

Mind grammar provides the means to think (and read and write) of subject matter critically. It provides the basis for moving the profession into far more effective practice. It paints on a different, critical, canvas than serialism-based instruction. It does away with the idea that new and revisited subject matter facts and ideas are something apart from critical thinking, reading, and writing. Once mastered, critical instruction and learning saves time. The instructional sets in Chapters 4 through 7 show how this is accomplished.

It takes time—but surprisingly little time—for both teachers and students to grasp and use critical instruction and learning. It is a matter of weeks, not months. One reason is that mind grammar is rooted in our innate ability to think critically. Such thinking is applied constantly in day-to-day life.[12] Another reason is that, for the first time, teachers and students can now share critical reasoning, reading, and writing strategies. Such sharing makes classroom assignments easier to understand and quicker to be completed. Consequences for teachers include greatly improved preparation and practice and for students, critical thinking, reading, and writing abilities and greatly improved achievement.

16. *Must an instructional set (classroom assignments) be developed for every topic I teach?*

To begin reading an answer to this question, see the answer to question 3 on subject matter displays and then return here. To continue, the mission statements of schools, colleges, universities, and programs often state that a primary goal is to show students how to think critically. The same is true of standards for faculty and students.[13] This makes teaching for critical thinking, reading, and writing the essential responsibility of teachers at all levels and in all disciplines.

But the institution, its programs, and its faculty must go beyond critical thinking, which is the first language art. Whether in or out of classrooms, critical thinking is conducted primarily in the context of reading, listening, writing, speaking, and observing. Therefore, regardless of your discipline and the educational level at which you practice, it is your professional responsibility to have students develop, use, and practice the language arts for topics in your discipline.

For example, you can design reading and writing assignments that pair itechniques with mind grammar strategy. When this is done, you provide students not only with the opportunity to engage in critical thinking but in critical reading and writing as well. So how often should you design critically conceived classroom assignments? The answer lies in knowing how well your students in your school, college, or program can practice all five language arts in the context of engaging new and revisited subject matter.

17. *Which parts of an instructional set do my students see?*

Usually, students see only the classroom assignments. However, when the instructional set includes teacher resources, such as a display or narrative, students may be given those at the completion of assignments.

THE CONSEQUENCES OF INSTRUCTIONAL SETS

The positive consequences of instructional sets based on mind grammar are as follows. They provide the means to actively engage students in new and revisited subject matter while concurrently developing their ability to think, read, and write critically. They provide teacher–educators with specific examples to show teacher-candidates how to design classroom assignments that make use of mind grammar instructional strategies and instructional techniques. Teacher-candidates and practicing teachers have the operating basis for designing classroom assignments that implement critical learning when engaging new and revisited subject matter.

Instructional sets provide professional developers with specific examples to show inservice teachers how to design classroom assignments that make use of mind grammar instructional strategies and instructional techniques. Inservice teachers and instructional designers have the operating basis for designing classroom assignments that implement critical learning when engaging new and revisited subject matter.

Instructional sets also allow teacher–educators, teacher-candidates, teachers, and professional developers to more readily assemble collections of critical learning materials to share, explore, and revise with colleagues. The sets also establish the basis for team teaching efforts and provide the basis for interdisciplinary study programs. The sets also provide principals, assistant principals, and other evaluators with examples of critical classroom instruction and critical learning.

A neutral consequence of instructional sets is that, initially, they take time to develop. However, with practice, the time needed to develop sets will diminish significantly.

QUESTIONS

1. Why is an instructional set prepared?
2. What is the procedure for developing an instructional set?
3. Based on your answers to questions 1 and 2, develop a three-stage MG1 subject matter display on the instructional set.
4. Based on your answer to question 3, develop a four-stage MG2 subject matter display on the instructional set.
5. Identify the different types of classroom assignments. Describe three of them.
6. When writing classroom assignments, to whom should you talk directly?
7. Identify five things to keep in mind when developing a subject matter display.
8. What is the basis for a mind grammar narrative?
9. Name three things to keep in mind when writing a mind grammar–based narrative.
10. What determines how much classroom time it should take to complete a mind grammar–based classroom assignment?

NOTES

1. A typical lesson plan outline includes (1) topic, (2) aim, (3) learning objectives, (4) materials, (5) motivation, (6) classroom instructional assignments (the focus of this book), (7) assessment, and (8) follow-up. When practicing critical instruction, the *objective of the subject matter topic* should be added to the lesson plan outline after the topic.

2. The terms *thinking*, *reading*, and *writing* should be taken to apply to think, read, write, listen, speak, and observe.

3. MG1 and MG2 represent explicit and formal critical reasoning strategies that reflect and develop the mind's innate and informal ability to think critically. MG1 and MG2 are used to think, read, and write critically when engaging new and revisited subject matter. For an in-depth discussion of MG1 and MG2, see *Preparation for Critical Instruction: How to Explain Subject Matter While Teaching All Learners to Think, Read, and Write Critically* (Maiorana, 2016b).

4. From this point on, a mind grammar instructional set will be referred to simply as an instructional set.

5. For a full discussion of (a) conventional rote-inducing serialism and its negative impact on teacher effectiveness and student achievement, (b) rote inducing-describing versus critical thinking inducing-explaining, and (c) critical reasoning strategies and critical skills development, see *Fixing Instruction: Resolving Major Issues with a Core Body of Knowledge for Critical Instruction* (Maiorana, 2016a).

6. Your author originated the concepts of subject matter universals and mind grammar and their application to engaging new and revisited subject matter.

7. For a full discussion of critical writing, see Chapter 8, Write for Critical Explanation, in *Preparation for Critical Instruction* (Maiorana, 2016b).

8. For a more in-depth discussion with students on mind grammar, you can draw on the material in *Preparation for Critical Instruction.* In particular, you can use material from Chapter 4, Introduction to Critical Learning; Chapter 5, Critical Understanding with Mind Grammar One; and Chapter 6, Critical Comprehension with Mind Grammar Two.

Tailored suitably to your students, you can also develop a version of "Subject Matter Speaks." See *Preparation for Critical Instruction*, page 41.

9. For more on the critical writing plan, see Chapter 8, Write for Critical Comprehension, in *Preparation for Critical Instruction.*

10. Such conventional viewpoints are traceable to the standard classroom practice of serialism-based instruction and learning, which induces rote learning and defeats the development of critical thinking, reading, and writing. See Examples of Istrategies in Chapter 1. For an in-depth discussion of the great limitations of serialism-based instruction, see Chapters 2, 3, and 6 in *Fixing Instruction.*

11. This limited view of subject matter was held by the noted educator John Dewey. For a discussion of his limited views on the nature of subject matter, see *Fixing Instruction*, page 48.

12. For more on the innate ability of the conscious mind to engage the world critically, see Chapters 3 and 6 in *Fixing Instruction* and the index entry "human mind, ability to reason" in *Preparation for Critical Instruction.*

13. See *Fixing Instruction* for a comprehensive discussion of the historic lack of critical instruction and learning regarding programs and standards for teachers and students.

BIBLIOGRAPHY

Maiorana, V. P. (2016a). *Fixing instruction: Resolving major issues with a core body of knowledge for critical instruction.* Lanham, MD: Rowman & Littlefield.

Maiorana, V. P. (2016b). *Preparation for critical instruction: How to explain subject matter while teaching all learners to think, read, and write critically.* Lanham, MD: Rowman & Littlefield.

Merriam-Webster's collegiate dictionary (11th ed.). (2007). Springfield, MA: Merriam-Webster.

Chapter Three

Mind Grammar Instructional Techniques

Subject Matter Objective: The function of a mind grammar–based instructional technique is to design classroom assignments that engage students with new and revisited subject matter while concurrently developing their ability to think, read, listen, write, speak, and observe critically.

Classroom assignments that produce the ability to think, read, listen, write, speak, and observe critically need two key resources: first, an instructional strategy based on a critical reasoning strategy and, second, an instructional technique that is paired with the critical reasoning strategy. That combination yields a critical instructional method.[1]

With mind grammar as the critical reasoning instructional strategy, twelve itechnique categories are discussed in this chapter. They are itechniques that introduce students to mind grammar–based critical learning, itechniques for incomplete subject matter displays, itechniques for critical writing, itechniques for critical reading, itechniques for english language learners, itechniques for students with limited skills, itechniques for problem solving, gamelike itechniques, itechniques for collaboration, still-deeper learning through exploratory itechniques, creative thinking itechniques, and computer-based itechniques.

Please keep these general points in mind when reading the itechniques:

- The itechniques described are based on the use of MG1 and MG2 mind grammar istrategy.
- When the phrase "elements of mind grammar" or "mind grammar elements" is used, it refers to subject matter objective, activities, consequences, and resources.
- Most itechniques require students to work at thinking, reading, and writing critically. This leaves you free to provide help to individuals or groups as needed.
- Most of the itechniques lend themselves to group work.

The itechniques in this chapter represent an ever-enlarging collection. You can adapt, revise, modify, or improve the itechniques as desired. Better still, you can create your own itechniques.

ITECHNIQUES THAT INTRODUCE STUDENTS TO CRITICAL LEARNING

Decide which of the following itechniques to use based on the grade level, topic, and nature of the students in your class. You may choose to use more than one introduction itechnique.

1. The Active Lecture

As with all the mind grammar itechniques, this itechnique can be used with any subject matter topic. In the following example, the human blood circulation system is the topic.

1. Select a topic and develop a mind grammar–based narrative. If you are experienced with mind grammar, you can write the narrative directly. If not, develop a subject matter display and use it as an outline for writing the narrative.
2. Write the topic on the board. Just beneath the topic, write the subject matter objective. Ask students to copy the title and objective into their notebooks at the top of a new page.
3. Tell the class you are going to explain the human blood circulation system.
4. Ask students to write down anything they hear that concerns a noun, that is, a person, place, thing, or idea. Emphasize the nouns as you speak.
5. Explain the topic critically. You can read the narrative directly or use it as a guide for your lecture. Upon completing your explanation, call on students to say which nouns they identified.
6. Have students form groups of three. Provide each group with a copy of the narrative. Have students read the narrative. Ask them to make a list (in their notebooks) of the activities described in the narrative. Otherwise, read the narrative again and ask students to listen and note the mention of activities.
7. Sketch or project a blank subject matter display on the board. Ask students to sketch the blank display in their notebooks. You may also hand out a blank display.
8. Have students connect and integrate their information by developing a three-stage MG1 subject matter display in their notebooks. They complete the display by using the title and subject matter objective they copied from the board, the notes on resources they recorded from your earlier discussion, and the activities they identified in their group work.

2. Conventional Classroom Discussion with Critical Summary

Conduct a conventional subject matter discussion. A conventional discussion presents facts and ideas without explicitly and formally attempting to connect and integrate them critically.[2] Upon completion, tell students you are going to reconstruct the discussion critically and they should take notes as you proceed. Then summarize the discussion on the board using a subject matter display.

3. Critical Classroom Discussion

Start the discussion by saying, for example, "Today we are going to discuss the cell. The function of the cell is to serve as the basic building block for a living thing. We are going to find out how that function is carried out." Then develop your discussion by using either MG1 or MG2 mind grammar. You will cover the same material usually covered. Your students will be exposed to the same facts and ideas, but there is one major difference between this discussion and a conventional discussion. You will have explained the subject matter within a critical reasoning context. In doing so, students are able to develop their ability to think critically. Upon completion, tell students you are going to review the discussion in a formal and critical manner. Then summarize the discussion on the board using a subject matter display.

4. Subject Matter Display in List Form—All Items Identified, Teacher Develops Display

Develop a list, in random order, of all the items in a subject matter display. Place a blank line to the left of each item in the list. On these lines, write in the mind grammar nature of each item. Use these codes: "t" (for the title), "o" (for the objective), "a" (for an activity), "cp" or "c+" (for a positive consequence), "cn" or "c–" (for a negative consequence), and "r" (for a resource).

Distribute the list. Describe briefly the nature of a subject matter objective, activity, resource, and consequence. Proceed down the list as you identify and explain the nature of each item. Then say you are going to show how to connect and integrate the list into a sort of word picture. The picture that results will represent a critical view of the topic. Develop the display on the board as students write the display into their notebooks.

5. Subject Matter Display in List Form—All Items Identified, Students Develop Display

Develop a list, in random order, of all the items in a subject matter display. Place a blank line to the left of each item in the list. On these lines, write in the mind grammar nature of each item. Use these codes: "t" (for the title), "o" (for the objective), "a" (for an activity), "cp" or "c+" (for a positive consequence), "cn" or "c–" (for a negative consequence), and "r" (for a resource). Distribute the list. Working on their own, or in groups, students develop a subject matter display based on the marked items.

6. Subject Matter Display in List Form—Items Not Identified

Develop a list, in random order, of all the items in a subject matter display. Place a blank line to the left of each item in the list. Distribute the list. Tell students that each item in the list represents a specific mind grammar element. Each item in the list represents either a subject matter objective, an activity, a resource, or a consequence. Describe briefly the nature of the four elements.

Select several items and decode them for the class. Use these codes: "t" (for the title), "o" (for the objective), "a" (for an activity), "cp" or "c+" (for a positive consequence), "cn" or "c–" (for a negative consequence), and "r" (for a resource). Students then decode the remaining items in the list. When decoding is complete, review each item and ask students to identify its nature. Then show students how to connect and integrate the items into a subject matter display.

7. Subject Matter Display Plus List of Missing Items

Distribute a display that includes the title and about 60 percent of the items in the complete display. You can leave out items from any part of the display (you decide). Also, distribute a list, in random order, of the missing display items. Place a blank line to the left of each item in the list. Students classify each item in the list as a subject matter objective, activity, consequence, or resource. As each item is classified, students write their answer on the corresponding blank line. These codes can be used: "o" (for the objective), "a" (for an activity), "cp" or "c+" (for a positive consequence), "cn" or "c–" (for a negative consequence), and "r" (for a resource). Once classified, students use their answers to complete the display. They can then write a narrative using the display as a writing outline.

8. Subject Matter Display, Students Supply Missing Items

Distribute a display that includes the title and about 60 percent of the items in the complete display. Leave out items from parts of the display. Students complete the display based on a classroom lecture and/or a reading assignment. They can then write a narrative using the display as a writing outline.

9. Scrambled Subject Matter Display

Provide students with a display in scrambled order. A scrambled display purposively misplaces the mind grammar elements within a display. For example, a resource is shown under activities, an activity appears as a subject matter objective, and the subject matter objective appears as a consequence. The display title can be placed anywhere. Describe briefly the nature of each mind grammar element. Point out and correct with the class one or two errors. Have students identify the remaining errors. Review findings by calling on students to cite an error and its correction.

10. Peer Review of Subject Matter Displays

Every instance of developing a subject matter display (such as in itechniques 1 through 9) provides an opportunity for peer review. After students develop a display by working on their own, place them in groups. Students review and comment on each other's work.

Itechniques 1 through 10 can also be used after students are familiar with mind grammar strategy.

ITECHNIQUES FOR INCOMPLETE SUBJECT MATTER DISPLAYS

11. Incomplete Subject Matter Display with Support Materials

Provide an incomplete display with several entries missing from each part of the display. Students develop the missing entries by referring to class notes.

12. Incomplete Subject Matter Display with No Support Materials

Provide an incomplete subject matter display with several entries missing from each part of the display. Students develop the missing entries based only on their knowledge of course material already discussed.

13. Missing Subject Matter Objective

Provide a display that lacks a subject matter objective. Students infer an objective that would lend itself to the activities, resources, and consequences provided.

14. Missing Activities

Provide a display that lacks activities. Students determine the activities. Provide these hints: (a) What activities would lead to achieving the objective? (b) How might the resources be used?

15. Missing Consequences

Provide a display that lacks consequences. Students develop positive and negative consequences based on achieving or not achieving the subject matter objective.

16. Missing Resources

Provide a display that lacks resources. Students develop the resources. Provide these hints: (a) What resources would be needed to achieve the subject matter objective? (b) What resources are implied or actually stated in the activities?

17. Finding Resources in Activities

Provide a list of related activities in logical order.[3] Ask students to make a list of all the resources they can identify that are either stated directly within the activity or can be inferred.

18. Resource Use

Students look at the resources in a subject matter display. Students place the resources in the order they would be utilized based on the associated display activities.

19. Resource Grouping

Students look at the resources in a subject matter display. Students group the resources according to some classification scheme that you provide, such as persons, places, things, ideas, alphabetical, hierarchical, and importance. Other classifications include order of use, social value, dollar value, size, and weight.

20. Resource Importance

Students look at the resources in a display. They list the resources in some stated order of importance.

ITECHNIQUES FOR CRITICAL WRITING

Every completed subject matter display represents an opportunity for critical writing. The display provides students with a seamless way to transition to writing. Note: When an itechnique calls for the use of a narrative, it means a narrative based on mind grammar strategy.

21. Critical Writing Using a Display Distributed in Class

Distribute a complete subject matter display. Have students follow along as they watch you translate the display into a critical narrative. Write the narrative on the board. Have students write the narrative in their notebooks. After a few such demonstrations you can ask students to work on their own and write narratives for displays they develop.

22. Display to Narrative

Distribute a display. Students use the display as an outline and write a narrative.

23. Critical Writing Using a Display Developed by Students

Have students develop a subject matter display. Students write a corresponding narrative in their notebooks. After a few such assignments, you can ask students to write narratives routinely for the displays they develop.

24. Incomplete Narrative Plus List of Missing Items

Provide a narrative with missing words or phrases. Place blank lines to represent the missing words or phrases. Distribute a list, in random order, that contains the missing words or phrases. Students use the list to complete the narrative.

25. Subject Matter Display with Incomplete Words

Distribute a display. The display is complete except letters are missing from at least 25 percent of the words. The incomplete words appear throughout the display. Place a blank line for each missing letter, as in miss _ _ _. Students complete the words.

26. Portfolio of Subject Matter Displays

Have students keep a portfolio of all their subject matter displays, narratives, and other critical works. Make the portfolio an integral part of the students' grade. To grade a portfolio, review its contents with the student to see how much progress has been made in becoming a critical thinker, reader, and writer.

ITECHNIQUES FOR CRITICAL READING

With mind grammar strategy, all textual material, in whatever form it appears, can be read critically. This means that the mind grammar reasoning strategy provides the means to understand, comprehend, and evaluate all textual material. Note: When an itechnique calls for the use of a narrative, it means a narrative based on mind grammar strategy.

27. Narrative to Display

Distribute a regular narrative. Students read the narrative and develop a display.

28. Partial Subject Matter Display Plus Narrative

Provide students with a partial subject matter display. Also, distribute a regular narrative.[4] A regular narrative contains a title plus all the mind grammar elements of subject matter objective, activities, resources, and consequences. Students read the the narrative, find the missing display items, and add them to the display.

29. Partial Subject Matter Display Plus Enriched Narrative

Provide students with a partial subject matter display. Also, distribute an enriched narrative. An enriched narrative contains all the basic mind grammar elements plus additional material that broadens the discussion and provides more detail.[5] Students read the narrative, find the missing display items, and complete the display.

30. Narrative with Words Misplaced

Provide a narrative in which words associated with the elements of subject matter objective, activities, resources, and consequences are intentionally misused within the narrative. Underline the misplaced words. Students read and correct the narrative and then develop a subject matter display.

31. Narrative with Out-of-Order Activities

Distribute a narrative that includes activities that are not in logical order. Students read the narrative, identify the activities, and then arrange them in logical order.

32. Peer Review of Narrative

Every instance of developing a narrative provides an opportunity for peer review. After students develop a narrative by working on their own, place them in groups. Students review and comment on each other's work.

33. Read for Understanding

Have students apply MG1 mind grammar for reading. The textual material can take the form of one or more paragraphs in a textbook, magazine or newspaper article, or digital material. Students will need to develop a specific subject matter objective for the material. They then use the subject matter display (or equivalent) they develop as a basis for writing a corresponding narrative. For a discussion on how to read for critical understanding, see Chapter 7 in *Preparation for Critical Instruction.*

34. Read for Comprehension

Have students apply MG2 mind grammar for reading. The textual material can take the form of one or more paragraphs in a textbook, magazine or newspaper article, or digital material. Students will need to develop a specific subject matter objective for the material and develop positive and negative consequences as well. They then use the subject matter display (or equivalent) they develop as a basis for writing a corresponding narrative. For a discussion on how to read for critical comprehension, see Chapter 7 in *Preparation for Critical Instruction.*

35. Read a Textbook Chapter for Understanding

Students apply MG1 mind grammar to reading a textbook chapter. If not evident, students will need to develop an explicit subject matter objective for the material. They then develop a three-stage subject matter display (or equivalent).[6]

36. Reading a Textbook Chapter for Comprehension

Students apply MG2 mind grammar to reading a textbook chapter. If not evident, students will need to develop a specific subject matter objective for the material as well as positive and negative consequences. They then develop a subject matter display (or equivalent).[7]

37. Evaluate Textbook Chapter

Assign a specific textbook chapter or have students select textual material. Have them identify which mind grammar elements they find missing in the material.

38. Evaluate Newspaper or Magazine Article

Teach your students what you have learned of information-loaded versus rhetoric-loaded subject matter.[8] Have your students analyze a newspaper or magazine article to determine whether the piece represents a well-founded discourse or a biased presentation.

39. Information-Loaded versus Rhetoric-Loaded Material

Teach your students what you have learned of information-loaded versus rhetoric-loaded subject matter.[9] Provide a sample of information-loaded text and a sample of rhetoric-loaded text. Have students develop subject matter displays for each. Have students identify intellectual weaknesses in each (i.e., which mind grammar elements may be missing). For each type of material, have students develop a list of warnings they would offer to someone reading or listening to each type of material.

40. Incomplete Subject Matter Display—Use of Familiar Textbook Chapter

Provide an incomplete subject matter display with several entries missing in each of the four categories of subject matter objective, activities, resources, and consequences. Have students add missing entries by referring to the class textbook.

41. Incomplete Subject Matter Display—Use of Unfamiliar Textbook Chapter

Provide an incomplete display of a textbook chapter with several entries missing in each of the four categories of subject matter objective, activities, resources, and consequences. Have students develop the missing entries by referring to the textbook.

42. Critical Listening—Media and Audiotapes

This itechnique takes mind grammar outside the classroom and uses it as a portable critical reasoning tool. Using news media or audiotapes, students listen to a news broadcast or audiotape, take notes, and assemble them into a subject matter display. They then write a narrative based on the display. For Free Public Domain Audio Recordings, visit https://librivox.org/.

43. Critical Observing—Life and Art

This itechnique takes mind grammar outside the classroom and uses it as a critical reasoning tool. Students observe and take notes on a street; rural, mountain, or coastal scene; or works of art such as an oil painting. They report their observations through the development of a subject matter display. They then write a narrative based on the display. See the instructional set The Painting *Big Ben* by Andre Derain in Chapter 5. To view paintings on a variety of subject matter topics, visit https://www.gallery-worldwide.com.

44. Mind Grammar Visualization

Students listen to a short discourse (an attempt at explanation, an argument being made, a point being offered) or read a short piece (an editorial, a newspaper column) and apply mind grammar critical reasoning strategy in real time. A visual image is constructed in the mind's eye in the form of the equivalent of a subject matter display (that is, the material heard or read is interpreted in terms of the elements of a subject matter display: title, subject matter objective, activities, resources, and consequences). Students then engage in a critical discussion, or they can be asked to write out their vision in the form of a subject matter display or narrative.

ITECHNIQUES FOR ENGLISH LANGUAGE LEARNERS

These itechniques are for use with English Language Learners. Suitably adapted itechniques that appear under the heading Itechniques That Introduce Students to Critical Learning can be used as well.

45. Introducing Mind Grammar Vocabulary for English Language Learners

Provide a chart with two columns. The first column is in the student's native language. It contains a vertical list of the terms *title*, *subject matter objective*, *activities*, *consequences*, and *resources*. The second column is blank and is used to translate the terms into English.

46. Review a Subject Matter Display Out Loud

Distribute a three-stage MG1 display written in the students' native language. Provide a blank line next to each display entry. Read the display out loud in the native language. Start with the title and work your way through the display. Read it slowly. Explain how the activities and resources are used to achieve the subject matter objective. Reread the display. Proceed to translate the display into English. Start with translating the terms *title*, *subject matter objective*, *activities*, and *resources*. Students write the translation into the associated blank line. Continue and translate each display item into English. As you translate each entry into English, students write the translation on its blank line.

47. Two Columns

Distribute a chart with two columns. The first column is in the students' native language. The vertical list includes the headings for each part of a display (title, subject matter objective, activities, consequences, and resources) as well as all associated items. The second column is blank. Students use the second column and translate the terms into English.

48. Incomplete Native Language Display—Missing Words in Native Language

Provide an incomplete display in the students' native language. Also, provide a list of the missing words in the native language. Students complete the display.

49. Incomplete Native Language Narrative—Missing Words in Native Language

Provide a native language narrative with missing words or phrases. Place blank lines to represent the missing words or phrases. Distribute a list, in random order, containing the missing words or phrases in the native language. Students use the list to complete the narrative.

50. Incomplete Native Language Display—Missing Words in English

Provide an incomplete display in the students' native language. Also, provide a list of the missing words in English. Students complete the display.

51. Incomplete Native Language Narrative—Missing Words in English

Provide a native language narrative with missing words or phrases. Place blank lines to represent the missing words or phrases. Distribute a list, in random order, containing the missing words or phrases in English. Students use the list to complete the narrative.

52. ELL Translation Chart for a Narrative

This chart has two columns. The first column is in the students' native language. It lists vertically the title and each individual sentence in a mind grammar–based narrative. The second column is blank and is used to translate the title and sentences into English.

INITIAL ITECHNIQUES FOR STUDENTS WITH LIMITED SKILLS

With these itechniques, it is best to start with a two-stage MG1 display (objective and activities). Then add a third stage (resources) to the display.

53. Teacher-Led Verbalization on a Daily-Life Topic—Students Observe

Use verbalization to introduce mind grammar to students with poor reading and writing abilities. Select a topic that is within the common experience of your students (e.g., brushing teeth, buying sneakers, listening to music). As you speak, develop a subject matter display on the board. The students do not read or copy anything into their notebooks.

54. Teacher-Led Verbalization on a Course Topic—Students Observe

Select a course topic. Develop a subject matter display on the board. To promote comparison, develop the display next to the one developed in itechnique 53. The students do not read or copy anything into their notebooks.

55. Teacher-Led Completed Subject Matter Display—Students Observe

Hand out and explain a display. Proceed carefully, starting with the title and subject matter objective. Stress that resources and activities are used to achieve the subject matter objective. The students do not read or copy anything into their notebooks. They simply follow along as you describe and explain the display.

56. Teacher-Led Completed Subject Matter Display—Students Take Notes

This technique is similar to verbalization. This time, students write in their notebooks. Conduct a discussion in which you develop the subject matter display on the board. To the extent possible, have students help you develop the display (e.g., ask for help in selecting a word to use). As you develop each part of the display on the board, have your students copy the material into their notebooks.

57. Teacher-Led Poster-Size MG1 Display

This is another technique you can use to discuss content with students with poor reading and writing abilities or if you want to create a game atmosphere with younger students. Prior to class, cut strips of paper about 2 inches by 6 inches. On each strip, in large lettering, write out a single subject matter objective. Write out each activity and each resource on individual strips.

Prepare a display template in poster size (2 feet by 3 feet). Hang the poster on the wall at the front of the classroom. You write the title of the display on the poster. Place each strip face down on a table. Have students select a strip. Ask each student in turn to identify the nature of his or her strip (objective, activity, or resource). After discussing the nature of the strip and getting the class to agree, have the student tape or otherwise affix the strip in its proper location on the poster.

58. Teacher-Led Tabletop MG1 Display

Instead of placing strips on a poster, per itechnique 57, the display is laid out on a tabletop. To strengthen the strips and make them durable, back them with cardboard.

Note regarding initial itechniques 53 through 58: Through use of these itechniques, students will gain confidence in their ability to think critically. At this point, you can transition to itechniques 1 through 10.

ITECHNIQUES FOR PROBLEM SOLVING

59. Teacher-Led Mind Grammar Problem Solving

This itechnique uses mind grammar to help solve problems. The teacher identifies a problem and leads the class through to a complete solution to the problem. On the board or on an overhead, the teacher shows the class how to complete parts A and B (see below) and translate the information to a blank display. The teacher then shows how to solve the problem within the context of the display by (a) solving the problem in the activities portion of the display and (b) determining positive and negative consequences of achieving the objective (solving the problem).

Part A: Read and Understand the Problem Information

The Situation: In this space, describe the situation from which the problem is drawn. This becomes the title of the display.

Problem Statement: In this space, state the problem to be solved. This becomes the subject matter objective.

Part B: Use a Display to Set Up a Solution to the Problem

Develop a subject matter display as a basis to solve the problem. The problem situation is the display title. The problem to be solved becomes the subject matter objective. The means (activities and resources) become the basis for identifying solutions. The consequences serve to identify the likely results of solving the problem. Engage students with the process. If more than one solution becomes apparent, then develop a parallel list of activities.

60. Student-Led Mind Grammar Problem Solving

Students take the lead and use itechnique 59 to solve another problem. Use this itechnique only after you have first demonstrated itechnique 59.

GAMELIKE ITECHNIQUES

61. Subject Matter Display in Scattered Form

Distribute a subject matter display in scattered form. Instead of placing items in a simple straight list, scatter them throughout the face of a page: upside-down, backward, vertical, horizontal, slanted, and so on. Ask students first to circle the subject matter objective and connect with separate lines and circles resources, activities, and consequences. Once connected and identified, have your students assemble the items into a subject matter display and then write a narrative.

62. Scrambled Subject Matter Display

Provide a display in which the elements of subject matter objective, activities, consequences, and resources are scrambled within the display. Have students find the errors, develop a correct display, and write a narrative.

63. Dictionary Games

Students randomly select five words from a dictionary. For each word, they write down the first two definitional entries that appear. Using the definitions as raw material, have the students identify the resources and activities within the material and enter them into a blank subject matter display. Using their imaginations, students develop an overall subject matter objective and consequences for the partial display they now have. Be prepared to be very accepting of the responses you receive. Evaluate these analyses based on their own internal consistency, not on what you might have done beginning at the same starting point. The most important factor is whether the display is consistent with its subject matter objective.

64. Crossword Puzzle

Distribute a crossword puzzle devoted to the treatment of a particular course topic. It can cover all of a display or only a portion of a display. When students complete the puzzle, they then identify elements of subject matter objective, activities, consequences, and resources. Once identified, students (a) assemble the elements into a blank subject matter display, or (b) enter the elements as appropriate into a partial display you provide.

65. Student-Developed Crossword Puzzle

Have students first develop a subject matter display. Based on the display, they develop a crossword puzzle. If you assign students different topics, they can then solve each other's puzzles as a class activity.

For other gamelike itechniques, see the topic heading Creative Thinking Itechniques below.

ITECHNIQUES FOR COLLABORATION

Many of the itechniques promote your students' abilities at working together. Here are several more that are wider in scope. Stress that collaboration within the team is as equally important as competition between teams.

66. General Group Work

Place students in groups and have them (a) develop a subject matter display from scratch, (b) complete a partially developed display, or (c) unscramble a completed display.

67. Students as Teachers

Place students in groups of four. Have them appoint a group leader. Students refer to a textbook or other textual material, and each group develops a subject matter display. Each leader writes his or her group's display on the board. Have leaders conduct a critique of each other's displays with the whole class.

68. Calling in the Search Squads

Place students in groups of four. Have them appoint a group leader. Each group member will be named "subject matter objective," "resources," "activities," or "consequences." Have students refer to a textbook or other written material. The students investigate the material for the mind grammar elements associated with their "names." Have each group assemble a subject matter display from their findings. Each group leader writes his or her team's display on the board. Ask the class to critique the displays.

69. Team Competition

This is meant as a term-long or semester-long project. Organize the class into teams. The teams will each have special names. The teams will compete against each other in two leagues. The name of one league is "The Critical National League." The name of the other league is "The Critical American League." Teams within each league will compete through content-based subject matter displays, narratives, and the other itechniques described above. You establish the rules for assigning the number of points a team gains through various critical thinking, reading, and writing activities. The teams that win in their leagues will receive extra credit on their final grade or will be rewarded in some other suitable fashion. Teams that do not win receive a lesser reward.

70. Mind Grammar World Series

This is a follow-up to the Team Competition itechnique described above. The teams that win in their leagues will play in the "Mind Grammar World Series." Members from those teams that did not reach the World Series will act not only as fans but also with you as umpires, calling the analytical "strikes" and "balls" of competing teams. Devise a special, content-based problem that requires critical thinking, reading, and writing. Consider extending this itechnique to include whole grades or the entire school.

71. Research Project

Ask students (individually or in groups) to select a topic for which they have an interest but of which they have little knowledge. Have them research[10] the topic and develop a four-stage MG2 subject matter display. Based on this research and the display, students write an essay.

72. Term Project

Assemble teams of students. Group students so each group contains students of varying abilities. Select one or more of the itechniques described in this chapter and design classroom assignments. Assemble an instructional set that represents a term-long project assignment.

STILL DEEPER LEARNING THROUGH EXPLORATORY ITECHNIQUES

Exploratory thinking concerns looking at a subject matter display and/or its individual elements and considering them from different viewpoints.

73. Establish a Mind Grammar Pathway to Still Deeper Learning

Have students select a subject matter display. They then select a resource or an activity within the display for which they develop a separate subject matter display. This is called a pathway to still deeper learning. Pathways can drill down to smaller and smaller aspects of a larger topic. Pathways can also look up to a greater topic of which the current display is a part. Both directions provide a new critical pathway for investigation and increased understanding/comprehension of the main topic.

74. Create a Mind Grammar Wave for Still Deeper Learning

A mind grammar wave is developed by turning a consequential statement into a new subject matter objective. For example, consequences for both information-loaded and rhetoric-loaded subject matter displays will often address moral, ethical, social, religious, political, and other concerns. Each of these provides the basis for a new subject matter objective. The new subject matter objective serves as a basis for developing a new subject matter display.

75. Framing Questions Based on a Completed Subject Matter Display

Have students complete a display. Ask students to develop a series of questions based on the display. Since the intent is to have students go beyond the obvious (that is, to go beyond what is already in the display), encourage questions of all sorts. For example, questions can refer to how certain resources were designed, developed, and produced, or who first engaged in a given activity, or what values are implicit in the way in which resources are utilized and activities carried out. The possibilities are endless, and this itechnique is meant to encourage such wide-ranging questioning.

76. Framing "What-If" Questions

Whichever mode of critical thinking is being used (i.e., mode 1, 2, or 3), the ability to ask or frame questions is a key characteristic of a critical thinker. The basic elements of mind grammar provide the basis for asking key questions that result in critical understanding or comprehension. Mind grammar also provides the basis for asking what-if questions. What-if questions are actually consequential in nature. *What* would happen (i.e., what are the consequences) *if* a given situation should arise? The "what-if" questioning itechnique based on mind grammar has a major advantage. It develops in students the ability to frame such questions within a critical framework.

Based on a partial or complete subject matter display that you provide or students develop, students then ask *What* would happen *if* an activity could not be performed, or a resource were not available, or an anticipated consequence did not develop?

77. Answering What-If Questions

Based on first having used itechnique 76, select the more interesting and challenging questions and either engage in a classroom discussion of possible answers or ask that the questions be answered as part of a written assignment.

78. A Display in Time

Using a completed display, have students explore the impact on a display and its elements if set in different time periods throughout the past and into the future.

79. A Display in Space

Using a completed display, have students explore the impact on a display and its elements if set in different places on Earth and in the universe.

80. A Display in Motion

Using a completed display, have students consider the impact on a display's elements if set physically in motion.

CREATIVE THINKING ITECHNIQUES

Creative thinking concerns discovering something new and being imaginative. Therefore, exploratory itechniques 73 through 80 are also creative in nature in that they encourage and require imaginative thinking. So do itechniques 81 through 86.

81. A Display with Only a Title

Supply a blank subject matter display with only a title. Have students use their imagination and complete the display. Be prepared to be very accepting of the responses you receive. Evaluate the displays based on their own internal consistency, not on what you might have done beginning at the same starting point. The most important factor is whether the display is consistent with its subject matter objective.

82. A Few Scattered Entries

Supply a subject matter display with a few scattered entries subject to wide interpretation. Then have students complete the display. Be prepared to be very accepting of the responses you receive. Evaluate these analyses based on their own internal consistency, not on what you might have done beginning at the same starting point. The most important factor is whether the display is consistent with its subject matter objective and the items supplied.

83. Imagine a Subject Matter Objective from Activities

Provide a list of activities. Ask students to develop a series of subject matter objectives that the activities might serve.

84. Imagine a Subject Matter Objective from Resources

Provide a list of resources. Ask students to develop a series of subject matter objectives that the resources might serve.

85. Imagine Activities from Consequences

Provide a list of positive and negative consequences. Students develop a series of activities relevant to the consequences.

86. Imagine a Plot and Write a Story

Provide students with a few resources and activities. Ask students to write a short story that makes use of all the resources and activities.

COMPUTER-BASED ITECHNIQUES

Use these itechniques to assign projects that require the use of a computer.

87. Word Processing Application

Students key in their handwritten subject matter displays and narratives and print them out as reports to you in memo format. Students keep copies of their printouts in their mind grammar portfolios.

88. Spreadsheet Application

Students count the number of words associated with each part of a subject matter display: title, subject matter objective, activities, resources, and consequences (positive and negative). They prepare a spreadsheet that shows the number of words in each part of the display. They calculate (a) the total number of words in the display; (b) the percentage of words in each part of the display; and (c) the percentage of resources by person, place, thing, and idea.

89. Graph Application

Students plot the results obtained through using itechnique 88. For example, a bar chart that shows the number of words in each part of a display or a pie chart that shows the percentage of words in each part of a display.

90. Database Application

Students develop a database in which each record represents a different subject matter display. Each record will contain these fields: name of course, title of the subject matter display, date developed, source of textual or other material, number of words in the display, and whether a corresponding narrative has been written.

91. Authoring Software

Students develop an interactive program that computerizes one or more of the itechniques in this chapter.

92. The Internet

Using the Internet, students engage an individual in a mind grammar–based discussion. The idea is to show the individual how to develop a subject matter display. Students prepare a report on their experiences.

INSTRUCTIONAL TECHNIQUES AND MIND GRAMMAR VOCABULARY

The itechniques described in this chapter use standard terms for the elements of mind grammar. These terms are subject matter objective, activities, consequences, and resources. Here are other terms that may be used instead of the standard terms. Provide these synonyms after students have become familiar with mind grammar strategy. Students can choose to adopt the synonyms, stay with the standard terms, or use equivalent terms they identify.

Subject matter objective: subject matter intent
Activities: actions, dynamic cause, dynamic means, procedure, process
Resources: static cause, static means
Consequences: aftereffects, outcomes, results

QUESTIONS

Different Itechniques

Develop, adapt, revise, modify, improve, or create at least one new itechnique for each of the following twelve itechnique categories in this chapter.

1. Itechniques that introduce students to critical learning
2. Itechniques for incomplete subject matter displays
3. Itechniques for critical writing
4. Itechniques for critical reading
5. Itechniques for English language learners
6. Initial itechniques for students with limited skills
7. Itechniques for problem solving
8. Gamelike itechniques
9. Itechniques for collaboration
10. Still deeper learning through exploratory itechniques
11. Creative thinking itechniques
12. Computer-based itechniques

Establish a New Itechnique Category

Establish a thirteenth itechnique category. Develop at least three new itechniques for the new category.

NOTES

1. See Chapter 1 for a discussion of how an instructional strategy and an instructional technique combine to form an instructional method.
2. A conventional discussion is also called serialism-based instruction. For a discussion of rote-inducing serialism-based instruction, see Chapter 2, Instructional Practice Is Inherently Weak: The Hidden Story, in *Fixing Instruction: Resolving Major Issues with a Core Body of Knowledge for Critical Instruction* (Maiorana, 2016a).
3. For a discussion on how logical thinking and critical thinking are related, see Chapter 3, Thinking: The First Language Art, in *Preparation for Critical Instruction* (2016b).
4. For a discussion on critical narratives and how to use the Critical Writing Plan writing, see Chapter 8, Write for Critical Explanation, in *Preparation for Critical Instruction.*
5. For an example of an enriched narrative, see Text Box 8.3 in *Preparation for Critical Instruction.* In this book, see Text Box 6.1 on percentages.
6. For a discussion on how to summarize a textbook chapter for critical understanding, see steps 1, 2, 4, 5, and 6 in Text Box 7.17 in *Preparation for Critical Instruction.*
7. For a discussion on how to summarize a textbook chapter for critical comprehension, see Text Box 7.17 in *Preparation for Critical Instruction.*
8. See Chapter 2, The Nature of Subject Matter and Mind Grammar, in *Preparation for Critical Instruction.* See also, Additional Teacher Resources, in Chapter 4 in this book.

9. See Chapter 2, The Nature of Subject Matter and Mind Grammar, in *Preparation for Critical Instruction.* See also, Additional Teacher Resources, in Chapter 4 in this book.
10. See topic heading Research Topic in *Preparation for Critical Instruction*, page 104.

BIBLIOGRAPHY

Art Gallery Worldwide. (2009). The place to find your art. Retrieved from https://www.gallery-worldwide.com/

Kilmer, J. (n.d.). Trees and other poems. Librivox. Retrieved from https://librivox.org/trees-and-other-poems-by-joyce-kilmer/

Maiorana, V. P. (2016a). *Fixing instruction: Resolving major issues with a core body of knowledge for critical instruction.* Lanham, MD: Rowman & Littlefield.

Maiorana, V. P. (2016b). *Preparation for critical instruction: How to explain subject matter while teaching all learners to think, read, and write critically.* Lanham, MD: Rowman & Littlefield.

Part II

THE PRACTICE OF CRITICAL INSTRUCTION

Chapter Four

Instructional Sets for the English Language Arts

Subject Matter Objective: The purpose of mind grammar–based instructional sets in the English language arts is to actively engage students in new and revisited subject matter while simultaneously developing their ability to think, read, listen, write, speak, and observe critically.

This chapter illustrates how to design instructional sets on a variety of topics for the English language arts. Each set contains a number of classroom assignments as well as teacher resources. The resources contain guides for using the assignments in class as well as additional instructional materials.

Included in this chapter are instructional sets on Let's Explore the Story of Jack and Jill, Let's Explore Further the Story of Jack and Jill, Introduction to Critical Learning, The Adverb, Introduction to Critical Learning for English Language Learners, Lincoln's Gettysburg Address in Spanish, and Critical Visualization. The chapter section Additional Teacher Resources contains subject matter displays on critical thinking, critical reading, critical writing, reading an editorial, Herman the Horse, and the comma. These displays may be used to develop instructional sets.

Application Assignments appear at the end of the chapter.

LET'S EXPLORE THE STORY OF JACK AND JILL

Assignment 1—Read the Story of Jack and Jill

Jack and Jill is the name of a nursery rhyme. You can read it now in Figure 4.1. In the story, "to fetch" means the same as "to get." "Crown" means the same as "head."

Figure 4.1

Jack and Jill went up the hill to fetch a pail of water. Jack fell down and broke his crown, and Jill came tumbling after.

Assignment 2—Why Did Jack and Jill Go Up the Hill?

Why did Jack and Jill go up the hill? Write your answer on the following line. Write a complete sentence in your notebook.

Assignment 3—Explore the Story to Find Resources

Now, read the story again. This time, look for all the nouns. Nouns are persons, places, or things that appear in the story. Another way to say "nouns" is to use the word "resources." There are six resources mentioned in the story. When you find a resource in the story, place a box around it. See the example in Figure 4.1. Now, box all the resources you see in Figure 4.1. Then write them on the following lines.

1. Jack 2. _______ 3. _______ 4. _______ 5. _______ 6. _______

Assignment 4—Explore the Story to Find Activities

Now, look for all the activities in the story. An activity is when some action takes place. There are four activities in the story. When you find an activity in the story, underline it. See the example above in Figure 4.1. Now, underline all the activities you see. Then write them on the following lines. Write them in the order they appear in the story.

1. Jack and Jill went up the hill 3. ______________________
2. ______________________ 4. ______________________

Assignment 5—Let's Make a Word Picture of the Story

Let's make a sort of word picture of the information in the story. The picture is called a subject matter display. The term "subject matter" is a general way to refer to the topics you study.

A subject matter display helps you to *connect* and *organize* your thoughts. The display helps you to *understand* what you read. The display helps you to *remember* what you read.

Your teacher will sketch a blank subject matter display on the board. Copy the blank display into your notebook. Now, complete the display using your answers to Assignments 2, 3, and 4.

Assignment 6—Yes, No, or Can't Tell?

The display you made in Assignment 5 shows all the facts in the story. A fact is something you can show (prove) is true. For example, it is a fact that the word "pail" appears in the story. It is a fact that the activity "Jack fell down" appears in the story.

Now, let's see if you can answer these questions. Use the display to help you answer. For each answer, enter yes, no, or can't tell on the lines.

1. Did Jack and Jill run to the top of the hill? ____________
2. Was there a water well on the hill? ____________
3. Was the pail ever filled with water? ____________
4. Did Jack fall down? ____________
5. Was the hill a steep hill? ____________
6. Did Jack fall down on the way up the hill? ____________
7. Did Jack survive his fall? [Did he live?] ____________
8. Did Jill follow Jack down the hill? ____________
9. Did Jill get hurt? ____________
10. Are Jack and Jill children? ____________

Teacher Resources

1. You may wish to spread the assignments over more than one class meeting.
2. Figure 4.2 shows the completed subject matter display for Assignment 5. In class, sketch a blank version of Figure 4.2 on the board. The blank version should contain *only* the title of the display (including the word "title") and the headings that appear after the numerals (1), (2), and (3).

Figure 4.2

Title: A Subject Matter Display of the Story of Jack and Jill

(1) **Why did Jack and Jill go up the hill?**
- o They went up the hill to get a pail of water.

(2) **What Activities Are Described?** (Write them in the order described in the story.)
- o They went up the hill
- o Jack fell down
- o Jack broke his crown
- o Jill tumbled after Jack

(3) **Resources (Persons, Places, and Things)**

o Jack	o Jill	o hill
o pail	o water	o Jack's head (crown)

3. Consider using Assignment 6 as a homework assignment. Upon completion of this assignment, provide students with a discussion along these lines.

> For Assignment 6, you should have answered "can't tell" to all the questions except for 4 and 8. For example, the story does not mention if Jack and Jill ran or walked to the top of the hill. So the answer to question 1, "Did Jack and Jill run to the top of the hill?" has to be "can't tell." The same "can't tell" or "can't prove it" answer also applies to questions 2, 3, 5, 6, 7, 9, and 10. Nothing said in these questions can be *proven* true because confirming information is not included in the story. Therefore, you cannot answer yes or no to any of these questions. However, the answer to questions 4 and 8 is yes. Who can tell me why?

4. For more on Jack and Jill, and other nursery rhymes, visit http://www.jillwindmill.org.uk/rhyme.htm and http://www.poetryfoundation.org/poems-and-poets/poems/detail/46974.

LET'S EXPLORE FURTHER THE STORY OF JACK AND JILL

Assignment 1—What Is a Consequence [konsa-kwens]?

Is there more to the story of Jack and Jill? To find out, we will explore the idea of a consequence.

A good thinker looks ahead and sees consequences. A consequence is what can happen after something else has taken place. Consequences go with everything in life. Consequences follow anything you set out to do. Consequences follow anything you do not do. There are always consequences.

Consequences can be likely and unlikely. They can be large and small. They can be good and bad. Other words for consequence are result, outcome, and impact. Table 4.1 shows some examples of consequences.

Table 4.1. Examples of Consequences

Situation	*Possible Consequences*
eat too much	can get sick, can weigh too much
sleep poorly	lack energy, cannot pay attention
play a game	can win, lose, gain skill, be injured
plant a tree	air cleansed, oxygen produced, shade provided
graduate high school and college	develop critical thinking, reading, and writing abilities; gain knowledge and self-esteem; get good job

Assignment 2—Think of Consequences

Let's practice thinking in a consequential way. Here are three situations. Write a good and bad consequence for each. Use your imagination. Write the answers in your notebook.

- Use a cell phone
- Ride a bicycle
- Watch television

Assignment 3—The Consequences for Jack and Jill

Here are five situations regarding the story of Jack and Jill. Complete the following three sentences. Use your imagination. Write and complete each sentence in your notebook. (a) A consequence of getting a pail of water is __________. (b) A consequence of not getting a pail of water is __________. (c) A consequence of Jack breaking his crown is __________. (d) If Jack and Jill did not bring back water, then __________. (e) If Jill had not gone up the hill, then __________.

Teacher Resources

1. For Assignments 1 and 2 you can, of course, add additional situations.
2. Regarding Assignment 3, let students know that their answers should follow from the situations described. In this respect, be very accepting of how students respond. As long as an answer, no matter how unusual, follows logically from a situation, then it is a valid consequence.
3. Consider designing an Assignment 4 where students identify situations from their individual everyday lives and then consider the good and bad (positive and negative) consequences.

INTRODUCTION TO CRITICAL LEARNING

Assignment 1—Get the Logic: Rain

- Step 1: Read the paragraph on rain in Text Box 4.1.
- Step 2: Read the paragraph again. This time underline all the activities in the paragraph. Hint: There is one activity in the first sentence. There are two activities in the last sentence. There are seven activities in the whole paragraph.
- Step 3: Make a list of the activities in your notebook. Number the activities 1 through 7.

Text Box 4.1

HOW IT RAINS

(1) Warm air turns the water from rivers, lakes, and oceans into water vapor. (2) The water vapor rises into the air. (3) That water vapor forms clouds, which contain small drops of water or ice crystals. (4) As clouds rise higher and higher, the air gets colder and colder. (5) When the water vapor in the cloud becomes too heavy, it falls back to the ground as rain or snow.

Assignment 2—Why Is Rain Important?

Look over the activities you listed in Assignment 1. Now, think about why rain is important to human beings. Write a complete sentence in your notebook. The sentence you write is called a subject matter objective.

Assignment 3—Put Your Ideas Together

In this assignment, we will use a subject matter display. A display helps you to connect and organize your thoughts. Turn to a new page in your notebook. Copy the blank display in Figure 4.3 into your notebook. Then complete the display using your answers to Assignment 2.

Figure 4.3

Title: A Subject Matter Display of Rain (Blank)

(1) **Importance of Rain** (Why is rain important from a human being's viewpoint)?
Write a complete sentence on these lines.

____

____.

(2) **Activities** (What are the activities that go with rain?)

o
o
o
o
o
o
o

Assignment 4—What Can Happen During and After It Rains?

To complete the subject matter display, we will now consider consequences. Consequences address what can happen—good and bad—after a subject matter objective has been achieved.

The paragraph in Assignment 1 does not address the consequences of rain. Think of some good and bad consequences of rain. Write them down in your notebook under your subject matter display. Use the heading "Some Consequences of Rain."

INTRODUCTION TO CRITICAL LEARNING FOR ENGLISH LANGUAGE LEARNERS

Assignment 1—The Vocabulary of Critical Learning

Copy Table 4.2 into your notebook. Follow your teacher as each term is translated into your first language. Write the translation into your notebook.

Table 4.2. Critical Learning Terms Translation Table

Term in English	*Term in Your First Language*
Title	
Subject matter objective	
Activities	
Consequences	
Positive	
Negative	

Assignment 2—A Critical View of the Hand

We will now take a critical view of the hand. Copy Table 4.3 into your notebook. Follow your teacher as each term is translated into your first language. Write the translation into your notebook.

Table 4.3. The Hand Translation Table

English	*Your First Language*
Title: A Subject Matter Display of the Hand	
(1) Subject matter objective:	(1)
A purpose of the hand is to hold objects.	
(2) Activities: think, reach, grasp	(2)
(3) Consequences:	(3)
Positive: The object can be used.	
Negative: The object can hurt hand.	
(4) Resources: brain, fingers, palm, object	(4)

Assignment 3—Let's Turn the Table into a Critical Learning Picture

We will now make a word picture of the information in Table 4.3 in Assignment 2. The picture is called a subject matter display. The term "subject matter" is a general way to refer to the topics you study.

A subject matter display helps you to *connect* and *organize* your thoughts. The display helps you to *understand* what you read. The display helps you to *remember* what you read.

Your teacher will sketch a blank subject matter display on the board in your first language. The blank version will contain *only* the title of the display (including the word "title") and the headings that appear after the numerals (1), (2), (3), and (4).

Copy the blank display into your notebook. Now, complete the display using your first language answers from Table 4.3 in Assignment 2.

Assignment 4—Translate the Subject Matter Display on the Hand into English

In Assignment 3, you completed a subject matter display in your first language. Now, translate the display from your first language into English. Write the display in your notebook.

Assignment 5—Write a Narrative on the Hand in English

In this assignment, write a narrative on the hand in English. Use the English language display you completed in Assignment 4 as a writing outline.

Teacher Resources

1. You may wish to translate the assignment instructions into your students' first language. You may also change the direction of the table (i.e., critical learning terms in first language, translation into English in the second column).

2. In their native language, introduce Assignment 1 on critical learning along these lines.

> Here is something important you should know. You were born with and have the natural ability to think critically. This is true regardless of your race, religion, gender, background, or first language. This means you already have within you the mental ability to be a critical learner. A critical learner wants to know the *why* of something. In other words, he or she wants to know the function, meaning, purpose, or importance (the objective of) of something. The something could be anything, including all the subject matter topics he or she studies in school. A critical learner also wants to know how things work (activities) and what value a topic can have in the future (consequences). In this assignment, we will discuss the vocabulary of critical learning.

THE ADVERB

Assignment 1—Read a Narrative on the Adverb

Read the narrative on the adverb in Text Box 4.2. As you read, underline each example of an adverb that appears in parentheses.

Text Box 4.2

THE ADVERB

Adverbs are similar to adjectives. Just as the adjective tells us more about nouns, the adverb tells us more about verbs. The function of the adverb is to describe a verb. To use an adverb, one must start with a complete sentence that contains an action verb. An action verb is a word that shows action (e.g., talk, walk, run, and climb).

Also needed is a desire to give more information by telling how, when, or where. For example, you need adverbs that tell *how* (e.g., slowly, rapidly, calmly), *when* (e.g., yesterday, later, tomorrow), and *where* (e.g., here, there, everywhere).

You can learn to use an adverb by first writing a sentence that contains an action verb but does not contain any adverbs (e.g., Mary will speak.). You can then add an adverb that tells *how* Mary will speak (e.g., Mary will speak *slowly.*). Next, you can add an adverb that tells *when* Mary will speak (e.g., Mary will speak slowly *tomorrow.*). Next, you can add an adverb that tells where Mary will speak (e.g., Mary will speak slowly tomorrow *here.*).

If adverbs are properly used, the reader or listener will better understand the situation being described. If adverbs are not used, or improperly used, the reader or listener will have less understanding of the situation being described.

Note: Other purposes of adverbs include modifying adjectives and modifying other adverbs. This discussion covers using only adverbs to modify verbs.

Assignment 2—Write Sentences That Include Adverbs

Write a series of sentences as follows. (1) Write a sentence that uses Mary and the word *sing*. (2) Write a second sentence and include an adverb that describes *how* Mary will sing. (3) Write a third sentence and include an adverb that describes *when* Mary will sing. (4) Write a fourth sentence and include an adverb that describes *where* Mary will sing. Now, write one sentence that describes how, when, and where Mary will sing.

Assignment 3—Rewrite a Portion of the Narrative on the Adverb

Repeat Assignment 2. Start with a sentence that includes the words *Ricardo* and *dance*.

Teacher Resources

Figure 4.4 shows a subject matter display on the adverb.

Figure 4.4

Title: A Four-Stage MG2 Subject Matter Display of the Adverb

(1) **What is the function of the adverb?**
o The function of the adverb is to give more information by describing a verb.*

(2) **How is the adverb used?**
1. Write a complete sentence containing an action verb, but which does *not* contain any adverbs.
   Example: Joseph *will walk.*
2. Add an adverb that tells how Joseph will walk.
   Example: Joseph *will walk slowly.*
3. Add an adverb that tells when Joseph will walk.
   Example: Joseph *will walk slowly tomorrow.*
4. Add an adverb that tells where Joseph will walk.
   Example: Joseph *will walk slowly tomorrow in the park.*

(3) **What are the results of using an adverb?**
Positive (if adverbs are used properly): The reader or listener will better understand the situation being described.
Negative (if adverbs are not used or used improperly): The reader or listener will have less understanding of the situation being described.

(4) **What is needed to use an adverb?**
o a complete sentence, o a desire or need to give more information by telling how, when, or where
o adverbs that tell *how* (e.g. slowly, rapidly, calmly)
o adverbs that tell *when* (e.g. later, yesterday, tomorrow)
o adverbs that tell *where* (e.g. here, there, everywhere)

Vocabulary Box:
Action Verb: A word that shows action (e.g. talk, walk, run, and climb).
Adverb: A word that further describes a verb.

* Note: Other ways of giving more information is to use adverbs to modify adjectives and to modify other adverbs. This display covers only using adverbs to modify verbs.

LINCOLN'S GETTYSBURG ADDRESS IN SPANISH

Asignación 1—Buscar los Recursos (Encontrar los Sustantivos)

Recuadro de texto 4.3 contiene discurso de Gettysburg de Lincoln. Leer y círculo de al menos diez recursos [personas, lugares, cosas, o ideas]. Trabajar con un socio.

Text Box 4.3

DISCURSO GETTYSBURG DE LINCOLN

19 de Noviembre 1863

[Traducido del Inglés.]

Hace ochenta y siete anos, nuestras padres fundaron en este continente una nacion nueva, concebida en la libertad, y dedicada al principio de que todas has personas son creadas iquales.

Ahora estamos envueltos en una gran guerra civil, tratando de averiguar si esta nacion, o cualquier otra nacion asi concebida y dedicado, puede durar mucho tiempo. Nos encontramos en un gran campo de batalla de aquella guerra. Estamos aqui para dedicar parte de aquel campo de batalla como lugar de descanso eterno para aquellos que dieron sus vidas para que la nacion pudiera vivir. Es apropiado y justo que hagamos esto.

Pero, en un sentido mas amplio, no podemos dedicar—no podemos consagrar—no podemos santificar—esta teirra. Los hombres valientes, vivos y muertos, que lucharon aqui la han consagrada, mas alla de nuestro pobre poder de aumentar o disminuir su valor. El mundo casi no notara ni recordara lo que estamos diciendo, pero no puede olvidar lo que ellos hicieron aqui. Los que sobrevivimos, por otro lado, tenemos que dedicarnos al trabajo por terminar que los que lucharon han llavado hasta aqui tan noblemente. Nos toca dedicarnos a la gran tarea que aun nos queda—que de estos condecorados muerto aumentemos nuestra devocion a aquella causa por la cual dieron la ultima prueba de su devocion—que aqui juremos que estos heroes no hayan muerto en vano—que esta nacion, bajo Dios, tenga un renacimiento de la libertad, y que el gobierno del pueblo, por el pueblo, para el pueblo, no desaparezca de la tierra.

Asignación 2—Encontrar las Actividades [Buscar Los Verbos]

Leer y subrayar todas las actividades (frases y oraciones que contengan verbos), en dirección de Gettysburg de Lincoln. Trabajar con un socio.

Asignación 3—Identificar la Intención (el objetivo) de la Discurso de Gettysburg de Lincoln

Leer la dirección otra vez. Ver también, sobre los recursos y las actividades desarrolladas en las Asignacións 1 y 2. ¿Que opinas fue el objetivo principal (es decir, el objetivo), de la discurso? Escriba una oración completa. Aquí están algunas maneras para comenzar la oración: (a) Discurso de Gettysburg de Lincoln es importante porque . . . , (b) el fin en vista del Discurso de Gettysburg de Lincoln es . . . , y (c) discurso de Gettysburg de Lincoln tiene significado porque . . . Seleccione uno de estos enfoques, o desarrollar su propio enfoque. Escriba su objetivo de la materia en tu cuaderno.

Asignación 4—Desarrollar Una Exhibición de Tres Etapas MG1 Materia

Basada en las Asignacións 1, 2, y 3, desarrollar una exhibición de materia MG1 de 3 etapas. Escribir la pantalla de su portátil. Asegúrese de que la pantalla tiene un título.

Asignación 5—Identificar las Consecuencias en la Discurso

Encontrar las consecuencias dentro de la Discurso. Entonces, actualizar la pantalla MG1 un MG2 pantalla añadiendo las consecuencias.

Asignación 6—Traducir Su Objeto Mostrar en Inglés

Traducir su MG2 exhibición de materia en inglés.

Teacher Resources

1. The reference for Lincoln's Gettysburg Address in English is *The Citizen's Almanac* (2014). U.S. Department of Homeland Security, Washington, DC, 2014, p. 33.
2. The subject matter display shown here in Figure 4.5 contains material that represents answers to both Assignments 4 and 5. It may be distributed to students after assignments have been completed. For more on Figure 4.5, see item 3 below.

Figure 4.5

Title: Una Visualizacion de la Materia del Discurso de Lincoln en Gettysburg 1863

(1) **¿Cuál es el fin en vista del discurso de Gettysburg de Lincoln**
o El fin en vista del discurso de Lincoln en Gettysburg es demostrar que los soldados en la batalla de Gettysburg no murieron en vano.

(2) **¿Qué actividades se describen en el Discurso de Gettysburg**
o nueva nación o sacada hace 87 años
o ahora participan en la gran guerra civil
o prueba de resistencia de la nación
o reuniendose para dedicar un cementerio
o terreno ya dedicado a los hombres valientes
o en cambio, deben tener un mayor dedicación a la causa
o debe resolver que los hombres no murieron en vano

(3) **Consecuencias**

Sacrificios del soldado daría lugar a un nuevo nacimiento de libertad; y que el gobierno de, por y para el pueblo no perecerá de la tierra.

Recursos (personas, lugares, cosas e ideas en la dirección)			
o años	o continente	o libertad	o devoción
o padres	o guerra civil	o tarea	o vive
o nación	o campo de batalla	o honrado muerto	o tierra nueva
o hombres (valiente, vivo, muerto, honrado)		o lugar de descanso final	o Dios
o gente (nosotros)		o tierra	o libertad
o creencias (todos los hombres son creados iguales)			o mundo
o gobierno de, por y para el pueblo			

3. The display in Figure 4.5 does not represent a single correct interpretation of the Address. See How to Tell If a Display Based on Rhetoric-Loaded Material Is Acceptable, under the heading Additional Teacher Resources.
4. For an English language version of Figure 4.5, see Figure 5.6.
5. For an English language version of this instructional set, see Lincoln's Gettysburg Address in English in chapter 5.

CRITICAL VISUALIZATION

Assignment 1—Read This Introduction to Critical Visualization

With practice, you can learn to apply mind grammar in real time. This means mind grammar can be used as a portable critical reasoning pattern as you seek to understand and comprehend material that is written, spoken, or observed. In other words, you apply mind grammar in real time as you read, listen, or observe. This will help you to evaluate if what you read, hear, and observe is fair-minded.

This is accomplished by cycling one's way through material using mind grammar–based reasoning. You form a mental image; you visualize the equivalent of a subject matter display. Whether found in a hard copy of a newspaper or on the Internet, the following assignments show how to apply critical visualization to an editorial or opinion piece.

Assignment 2—How to Read an Editorial Using Critical Visualization

You can read editorials to learn how to engage in mind grammar visualization. As you read an editorial, do the following:

1. Read to find the purpose of the editorial. The purpose will often appear in the headline or in the first sentence or paragraph. If the purpose is not immediately clear, go on to step 2.
2. Identify the information given to support the editorial's viewpoint (look for support in the form of facts and actions—resources and activities).
3. Look for consequences associated with the viewpoint being advocated. Has the editorial writer considered the consequences of what is being advocated for the idea, affected people, or institutions involved?

4. As you read an editorial for the above mind grammar elements, try to develop in your mind's eye the visual equivalent of the elements of a mind grammar display: subject matter objective, activities, consequences, and resources.

Assignment 3—Read an Editorial Using Critical Visualization

1. Your teacher will (1) provide you with a hard copy of an editorial, or (2) direct you to an Internet site that contains an editorial, or (3) otherwise provide or direct you to other resources.
2. Apply the four steps shown in Assignment 2 to the editorial.

Assignment 4—Review Your Critical Visualization

Form groups of three. Each person will take a turn identifying the mind grammar elements identified in the editorial as per Assignments 2 and 3. As a group, decide whether the editorial represents (a) a persuasive and fair-minded treatment of the topic, (b) a one-sided and biased treatment of the topic, or (c) something between (a) and (b).

Assignment 5—Think of the Consequences of Critical Visualization

Form groups of three. Make a list of the consequences, positive and negative, of applying critical visualization to an editorial.

Teacher Resources

Introduce students to critical visualization along these lines:

> The assignments in this instructional set demonstrate how you can use mind grammar as (1) a real-time portable critical reasoning strategy, (2) a way to assess in real time the critical thinking in one's self and in others, and (3) a way to build confidence in one's ability to think critically for comprehension in real time. This instructional set is an example of how all three ideas come together.
>
> The assignments in this set use the written editorial as an application example. However, in whatever medium you encounter them, you can apply critical visualization to editorials or opinion pieces (whether written or spoken); news reports; letters to the editor; Internet comments; radio, television, and Internet programs; and talk shows, panel discussions, and blogs. Mind grammar visualization also applies to your conversations on issues as well on things you observe, such as human behavior, photographs, and works of art.

ADDITIONAL TEACHER RESOURCES

How to Tell If a Display Based on Rhetoric-Loaded Material Is Acceptable

There should be little or no disagreement with the activities and resources shown in Figure 4.5. They do appear in the Address. However, when dealing with rhetoric-loaded material, the subject matter objective and consequences are open to interpretation.

The subject matter objective and consequences shown in Figure 4.5 represent one way of interpreting the Address. It does not have to be your view or the view of any of your students. Subjective interpretations are possible with all rhetoric-loaded material.

So how can you tell if a student has constructed an acceptable display that is based on rhetoric-loaded material? Here is the test. If the student's subject matter objective is reasonably supported by the activities described, then the display is most likely acceptable. If the consequences are a logical result of the stated objective, then the consequences are most likely acceptable. So bear in mind that it is not how you personally would interpret rhetoric-loaded material; it is whether the student has stated a reasonable subject matter objective and whether the activities and consequences that follow are true to the stated objective.

For more on the nature of subject matter, including rhetoric-loaded materials, see chapter 2, The Nature of Subject Matter and Mind Grammar, in *Preparation for Critical Instruction* (Maiorana, 2016).

Here are several subject matter displays on a variety of topics (Figures 4.6–4.10). They may be used as the basis for designing classroom assignments and assembling them into an instructional set. Use them to design classroom assignments by pairing them, as you see fit, with the instructional techniques discussed in Chapter 3.

A Subject Matter Display of the Three Modes of Critical Thinking

Figure 4.6

Title: A Four-Stage MG2 Subject Matter Display of the Three Modes of Critical Thinking

(1) **What is the end in view of critical thinking?**

o The end-in-view of critical thinking is to understand, comprehend, and explain new and revisited subject matter; defend or seek agreement on some issue, and to solve problems.

(2) **What are the main activities of critical thinking?**

Mode 1 - Understand, Comprehend, and Explain New and Revisited Subject

Understand and Comprehend

- o Select a topic
- o Obtain reading material and/or gather notes from a classroom lecture
- o Develop a MG1 subject matter display for understanding, or an MG2 display for comprehension.
- o Write a narrative based on your MG1 or MG2 display

Explain

- o Select a specific subject matter topic
- o Select a critical reasoning strategy to explain the topic (MG1 or MG2)
- o Develop a subject matter display (or equivalent) and/or write a narrative
- o Design Classroom assignments using mind grammar instructional techniques
- o Assemble assignments into an instructional set
- o Use, Assess, and revise the instructional set

Mode 2 - Argumentation

- o Identify and agree on an issue to be debated
- o question, defend, or seek agreement on the issue using argumentation strategies

Mode 3 - Problem Solving

- o Select strategy (scientific or conditional)
- o Select appropriate scientific or problem-solving procedure

o Carry out procedure
o Evaluate results

(3) **Consequences of engaging in the three modes of critical thinking**
Positive (if end-in-view of critical thinking is achieved):

For understanding, comprehending, and explaining: The knowledge gained critically can be put to use in school, in life, on the job, and when engaging in argumentation and problem solving.

For argumentation: issue resolved, subsequent actions based on agreement
For solving problems: situation resolved, person / organization can move forward.

Negative (if end-in-view of critical thinking is not achieved):
For understanding: ignorance continues.
For argumentation: issue not resolved, other viewpoints not appreciated; disagreement prevails.
For solving problems: problem continues to exact its tolls; future progress limited.

(4) **Resources** (the persons, places, things, and ideas needed to engage in the three modes of critical thinking).
o a person or persons o a desire or need to understand, comprehend, explain, debate, or problem solve.
o *For understanding, comprehending, or explaining: a* subject-matter topic, critical reasoning strategies for understanding, comprehending, and explaining new or revisited subject matter
o *For argumentation:* a topic for debate, debaters, debating strategies and skills
o *For problem solving:* a problem to solve, problem solvers, a problem-solving procedure

Vocabulary Box
Understand: To understand is to recognize the effect-cause or ends-means relationships that exist within a topic.

Comprehend: To comprehend is to recognize the effect-cause or ends-means relationships that exist within a topic and to then consider the consequences that follow.
Explain: To identify the objective of the topic, show how that objective is achieved, and then consider the consequences of achieving or not achieving the topic's objective.
Argumentation: To present one's viewpoint or debate another on an issue.
Problem solving: To Address conditional or scientific situations that require resolution.

Note. This subject matter display emphasizes Mode 1 of critical thinking. For more information on the three modes of critical thinking, see Chapter 3, Thinking: The First Language Art, in *Preparation for Critical Instruction – How to Explain Subject Matter While Teaching All Learners to Think, Read, and write Critically* (Maiorana, 2016).

A Subject Matter Display of Reading for Critical Comprehension

Figure 4.7

Title: A Four-Stage MG2 Subject Matter Display of Reading for Critical Comprehension

(1) **What is the purpose of reading for critical comprehension?**
o The purpose of reading for critical comprehension is to draw from the text the objective, processes, and consequences of the subject matter topic at hand.

(2) **Reading Activities**
1. Obtain the material to be read.
2. Read the first sentence in each paragraph.
3. Return to the first paragraph. This time do the following:

a. Place a check mark next to the phrase or sentence that represents the objective (i.e., the end-in-view, effect, meaning, importance, purpose, or function) *of the subject matter topic* discussed in the paragraph. The phrase or sentence you mark forms the basis for writing a subject matter objective. If the subject matter objective is not readily apparent, come back to it later.

b. Place a wavy line under phrases that represent activities.

c. Draw boxes around words that represent resources (persons, places, things, or ideas). It is alright to draw a box around a resource that appears within an activity that is already underlined. See example in Figure 8.1.

d. Mark with an "x" the phrases that represent consequences.

Note: This marking system is for use only when first learning to read for critical comprehension. For more on marking text, see Questions and Answers Regarding Critical Instruction Practice, in Chapter 2.

4. Transfer the subject matter objective, activities, consequences, and resources from the marked material to a 4-stage, MG2, subject matter display. If a subject matter objective has not become apparent within the text, then you will need to develop one. Base it on the parts of the display that you have already developed.

5. Assess the display for completeness. For example, if the textual material does not include a discussion of consequences, develop them yourself. When you enter your own consequences on the display, identify them as such. Use a comment such as "Consequences added."

(3) **What are the consequences of reading for critical comprehension?**

Positive for Reader: Reader is able to apply a critical reasoning strategy to (1) gain critical comprehension of textual material, (2) take intellectual charge of material, (3) recognize material that is written poorly, (4) all text, regardless of topic, can be read and evaluated critically.

Negative for Writer: The reader has the ability to assess the degree to which the writer has used a critical reasoning strategy to explain a topic.

(4) **Resource Bank** (persons, places, things, and ideas)
o reader o textual material
o the four universal attributes of subject matter (objective, resources, activities, and consequence)
o mind grammar strategy

Note. For more information on reading for both critical understanding comprehension, see Chapter 7, Read for Critical Comprehension, in *Preparation for Critical Instruction – How to Explain Subject Matter While Teaching All Learners to Think, Read, and write Critically* (Maiorana, 2016).

A Subject Matter Display of Writing for Critical Comprehension

Figure 4.8

Title: A Four-Stage MG2 Subject Matter Display of the Writing Plan for Critical Explanation

(1) **The purpose of writing for critical explanation**

o A purpose of writing for critical explanation is to use mind grammar to identify, connect, and integrate critically the four universal attributes of subject matter for a given topic.

(2) **The Critical Writing Plan for Critical Explanation**

A. Select topic.
  1. Identify topic
  2. State thesis
  3. Write subject matter objective
  4. Consider audience

B. Develop critical writing outline based on mind grammar critical reasoning strategy.
  1. Topic Title
  2. Topic Thesis Statement
  3. Topic Subject Matter Objective
  4. Topic Activities
  5. Topic Consequences
  6. Topic Resources

C. Research

D. Write draft using critical outline as a writing guide

E. Revise

F. Edit

G. Proofread

H. Distribute

(3) **What are the consequences of writing for critical explanation?**

Positive: (1) writers have the means to engage in the necessary critical thinking required when writing for critical explanation. (2) A document that is critically conceived and written. (3) The reader can achieve critical understanding and comprehension of a topic.

Neutral: Critical writing for explanation is more demanding than mere logical writing. It takes effort. It takes time. However, the result is a greatly superior explanation of the topic.

4. **Resource Bank** (persons, places, things, and ideas)
o writer o an outline critically conceived
o topic o sources of information
o subject matter objective for topic o audience
o the four universal attributes of subject matter (objective, resources, activities, and consequence)
o mind grammar strategy

Note. For more information on writing for critical explanation, see Chapter 8, Write for Critical Explanation in *Preparation for Critical Instruction – How to Explain Subject Matter While Teaching All Learners to Think, Read, and write Critically* (Maiorana, 2016).

A Subject Matter Display of Herman the Horse

Figure 4.9

Title: A Three-Stage MG1 Subject Matter Display of Herman the Horse

(1) **Why is Herman the Horse Important?**

o Herman the horse is important because he helps his owner to travel, hunt, and work.

(2) **What Actions or Activities Are Associated with Herman the Horse?**

o travels long distances
o runs around the farm
o helps people hunt
o follows commands
o learns his tasks
o works on farm
o coat grows thick in winter
o sheds hair in spring
o coat repels water

<u>Alternate Arrangement of Activities</u>

Physical
  o travels long distances
  o runs around farm
  o helps people hunt
  o works on farm
Mental
  o learns his tasks
  o follows commands
Natural
  o grows thick coat every winter
  o sheds hair in spring
  o repels water with coat

(3) **Resources** (What persons, places, things, and ideas are associated with Herman the horse?)

o Herman, the horse	o coat	o work
o owner	o winter	o tasks
o farm	o hair	o commands
o people	o spring	
o tasks	o water	

Vocabulary Box
horse: A large hoofed mammal having a shorthaired coat, a long mane, and a long tail,
mammal: a warm-blooded, back-boned animal characterized by a covering of hair on the skin.
hooves: the bone-like hard material that covers the toes or lower part of the foot of some mammals.
mane: the long hair along the top and sides of the neck of certain mammals.
shed: to have something fall off.

A Subject Matter Display of the Comma

Figure 4.10

Title: A Three-Stage MG2 Subject Matter Display of the Comma [,]

(1) **What is the function of a comma?**

o The function of a comma is to improve clarity in a written passage.

(2) **How is a comma used?**

o Write a passage.
o Look for the following instances in the passage:
  - Look for instances of <u>noun of direct address</u>. Insert comma as shown.
    Joe, open the door.
  - Look for instances of <u>coordinating conjunction</u>. Insert comma as shown.
    I thought John was present, but I was mistaken.
  - Look for instances of <u>introductory word group</u>. Insert comma as shown.
    Despite her numerous disabilities, Helen Keller was successful.

(3) **What consequences are associated with using a comma?**

Positive: Reader of the written passage better understands the communication.
Negative: Misuse of a comma can confuse a reader of the passage.

(4) **Resources** (What does one need to use a comma?)

o a desire or need to clarify writing
o a written passage
o symbol for the comma [,]

APPLICATION ASSIGNMENTS

The assignments below call for the design of instructional sets. Develop a four-stage MG2 subject matter display (or its mind grammar equivalent) as the basis for designing the set's classroom assignments. When designing the classroom assignments within a set, (1) select or adapt the instructional techniques from those given in chapter 3 or create your own original instructional techniques; (2) include at least three assignments in each set; and (3) engage students in some combination of thinking, reading/speaking, writing/listening, and observing for critical understanding and/or comprehension using the MG1 and/or MG2 reasoning strategy of your choice.

1. [A Fairy Tale]

Develop an instructional set for a fairy tale that you select. Use the instructional sets on Jack and Jill at the beginning of this chapter as a guide.

2. [Sign Language]

Develop a four-stage MG2 display on sign language. Use the display as a basis for developing an instructional set. For help on developing the display, visit www.lifeprint.com. Scroll down and read the essay "Hello ASL Heroes!" for MG2 critical comprehension. For help on reading for critical comprehension, see Figure 4.7, A Four-Stage MG2 Display of Reading for Critical Comprehension. For more information on reading critically, see chapter 7, Read for Critical Comprehension, in *Preparation for Critical Instruction* (Maiorana, 2016).

3. [Food]

Develop a two-stage MG1 display of food and use it to develop an instructional set.

4. [Critical Thinking]

Develop an instructional set based on the display on critical thinking in Figure 4.6.

5. [Critical Reading]

Develop an instructional set based on the display on critical reading in Figure 4.7.

6. [Critical Writing]

Develop an instructional set based on the display on critical writing in Figure 4.8.

7. [The Library]

Develop an instructional set based on the compressed subject matter display on the library shown here in Figure 4.11.

Figure 4.11

Title: A Four-Stage MG2 Subject Matter Display of a Library (Compressed)
(1) **Why is the library important?** o The library is important because it serves as a source of information in multi-media form; a place to do research, browse, and explore; and a place to read and study. (2) **Library Activities** o identify a topic of interest o ask librarians for help o do bibliographic research / browse stacks and digital resources o obtain materials o read materials and take notes o make record of sources used in bibliographic form (3) **Consequences of Using the Library** Positive: Understanding of the world is broadened, information for term paper and other assignments is obtained, knowledge of current events is improved, personal growth is enhanced, understanding of a library's resources improved. Negative: Understanding of world can remain narrow, term papers and other projects can be poorly supported, knowledge of subjects can remain dated. (4) **Library Resources** o librarians, o library catalog, o printed, digital, and audio-visual materials o computers o study corrals o time

8. [Herman the Horse]

Develop an instructional set based on the display on Herman the Horse in Figure 4.9.

9. [The Comma]

Develop an instructional set based on the display on the comma in Figure 4.10.

10. [Instructional Set]

Develop an instructional set on the instructional set.

11. [A Topic You Select]

Develop an instructional set for a topic you select.

12. [A Pathway to Deeper Comprehension]

A mind grammar pathway allows one to achieve deeper critical knowledge of a given topic. To develop a pathway, any entry within an existing subject matter display is selected. Then a new subject matter display for that entry (topic) is developed. The new subject matter display provides the basis for developing a new instructional set. Select any entry from within any of the subject matter displays in this chapter and develop an instructional set for it.

BIBLIOGRAPHY

Jack and Jill. Poetry Foundation. Retrieved from http://www.poetryfoundation.org/poems-and-poets/poems/detail/46974

Maiorana, V. P. (2016). *Preparation for critical instruction: How to explain subject matter while teaching all learners to think, read, and write critically*. Lanham, MD: Rowman & Littlefield.

SpanishDict. Retrieved from http://www.spanishdict.com

The Nursery Rhyme. Jack and Jill Windmills Society. Retrieved from http://www.jillwindmill.org.uk/rhyme.htm

U.S. Department of Homeland Security. (2014). *The citizen's almanac*. Washington, DC.

Vicars, W. (2015). Hello ASL heroes! American Sign Language University. Retrieved from www.lifeprint.com

Chapter Five

Instructional Sets for the Humanities

Subject Matter Objective: The purpose of mind grammar–based instructional sets in the humanities is to actively engage students in new and revisited subject matter while simultaneously developing their ability to think, read, listen, write, speak, and observe critically.

This chapter illustrates how to design instructional sets on a variety of topics for the humanities. Each set contains a number of classroom assignments and teacher resources. The resources contain guides for using the assignments in class and additional instructional materials.

Included in this chapter are instructional sets on A Wild Style of Painting, The Painting *Big Ben* by Andre Derain, Music, Listen to a Poem, The Battle of Gettysburg, and Lincoln's Gettysburg Address in English. The chapter section Additional Teacher Resources contains subject matter displays on perspective in drawing and philosophy. These displays may be used to develop instructional sets.

Application Exercises appear at the end of the chapter.

A WILD STYLE OF PAINTING

Assignment 1—A Wild Style of Painting

Andre Derain, a French painter, is famous for the style known as fauve. In the French language, the term *fauve* means wild beast. Figure 5.1 contains a narrative on the fauve, or wild, style of painting. You can read it now. For the moment, ignore the marked text.

Figure 5.1

A Wild Style of Painting

In a fauve painting, the artist uses vivid and pure colors √to show intense feeling for the subject. The artist decides on a subject to paint. The artist selects colors that do not naturally relate to the subject. The work of art is created by dabbing on the paint using contrasting pure unmixed colors.

A fauve artist also employs a flat pattern, uses bold brush strokes to harmonize the colors, and the paint is applied quickly. Andre Derain liked to paint bridges. He favored orange, blue, and red colors.

Assignment 2—What Is the Objective of the Wild Style of Painting?

The topic of the narrative in Assignment 1 is A Wild Style of Painting. The objective of this style of painting is given in the first sentence. It begins with the word "to" (see check mark in Figure 5.1). A subject matter objective is stated in a complete sentence. Therefore, the objective of the topic may be stated as follows: The end-in-view of the fauve painting style is to show the artist's intense feeling for a subject.

Turn to a blank page in your notebook. On the first line write: What is the end-in-view of the fauve painting style? On the second line write: The end-in-view of the fauve painting style is to show the artist's intense feeling for a subject.

Assignment 3—List the Activities That Appear in the Narrative

Look for the activities in the narrative in Assignment 1. An activity is when some action takes place. There are ten activities mentioned in the narrative. One activity is underlined.

Skip a line on your notebook page and copy Table 5.1 into your notebook. Head the table "Activities." Locate the activities that appear in the narrative. Underline each one. Then write the activities into Table 5.1. The first two and last activities have already been entered.

Table 5.1. Activities

1. uses vivid and pure colors	6.
2. decides on a subject to paint	7.
3.	8.
4.	9.
5.	10. Derain favored orange, blue, and red colors.

Assignment 4—List the Resources That Appear in the Narrative

In the Assignment 1 narrative, notice that the words "fauve painting" appear within a box. These words represent nouns, or persons, places, things, or ideas. Nouns can also be called resources. There are fourteen resources mentioned in the narrative.

Skip a line on your notebook page and copy Table 5.2 into your notebook. Head the table "Resources." Locate the resources that appear in the narrative. Draw a box around each one. Then write the resources into Table 5.2. The first two and last resources have already been entered.

Table 5.2. Resources

1. fauve painting	8.
2. artist	9.
3.	10.
4.	11.
5.	12.
6.	13.
7.	14. orange, blue, and red colors

Assignment 5—Review and Title Your Notes

Your notes should now contain three groups of entries: subject matter objective, activities, and resources. These entries represent a critical view of the topic. The view is called a subject matter display. Each display must have a title. At the top of your notebook page write "Title: A Subject Matter Display on the Fauve (Wild) Painting Style."

Teacher Resources

1. This instructional set may be used to introduce students to MG1 reasoning strategy.
2. For more on Fauvism, see http://www.metmuseum.org/toah/hd/fauv/hd_fauv.htm.
3. The subject matter display shown below in Figure 5.2 may be distributed to students (hard copy, screen projection, or digitally) after students have completed

Figure 5.2

Title: A Three-Stage MG1 Subject Matter Display of the Fauve Painting Style

(1) **What is the end-in-view of the Fauve painting Style? (What is the Subject Matter Objective?)**
- o The end-in-view of the fauve painting style is to show an artist's intense feeling for a subject.

(2) **What conditions, processes, actions, or operations are used in the Fauve painting style?**
- o The artist decides on a subject to paint.
- o Vivid and pure (unmixed) colors are used that do not naturally relate to the topic.
- o Paint is dabbed on using unmixed and contrasting colors.
- o Bold brush strokes are used to harmonize the colors.
- o Paint is applied quickly.
- o Subject matter is shown in a flat pattern to emphasize bluntness

(3) **Resources Needed for a Fauve Painting**
o A Fauve artist such as Andre Derain (A French fauve artist who liked to paint bridges and who favored orange, blue, and red colors.)

o A subject	o intense feeling	o flat pattern
o brushes	o vivid and pure colors	

Vocabulary Box
Fauve: A French term that means wild beast.

Assignments 1 through 5. Point out that the activities in Figure 5.2 are not listed in the order they appear in the Assignment 1 narrative. They have been rearranged to represent a more logical process. Notice that the resource box contains a mini-biography of Andre Derain.

Avoid suggesting that this display represents the only correct answer to Assignments 1 through 5. Variations are acceptable as long as they are consistent with the original textual material and with the proper application of mind grammar.

THE PAINTING *BIG BEN* BY ANDRE DERAIN

Assignment 1—Locate Andre Derain's *Big Ben* Painting

In these assignments, a whole painting, *Big Ben* by Andre Derain, serves as our subject matter. We will apply three-stage MG2 critical reasoning to the painting. We will start by locating a copy of the painting. Search the Internet using the term "andre derain big ben." You will be provided with many search results including this one: https://www.artsy.net/artwork/andre-derain-big-ben.

Assignment 2—What Is the Objective of the Painting *Big Ben*?

You will come across discussions of subject matter in many mediums that do not make clear the intent of the subject matter. This is often the case with works of art.

If Andre Derain were alive today, we could ask him directly: "Mr. Derain, what is the meaning of your painting?" It's possible that he may not be able to answer such a direct question because he may have just followed a creative burst of energy. So this leaves us with having to infer for ourselves the intent or meaning of the painting's subject matter.

We can begin with the name of the painting, *Big Ben*. But we cannot be sure if Derain or someone else provided the name. This leaves us with the painting itself. When viewing or observing the painting, we can see that the Big Ben clock tower is the most prominent feature of the painting. So perhaps we can use this as the basis for determining the painter's intent.

Accordingly, we could say, that the end-in-view of the painting *Big Ben* appears to be to depict the Big Ben clock tower and its surroundings in London, England. We do not know if this is true, but it is not an unreasonable statement. However, if you have another view of the painter's intent, then use your idea. Go ahead and develop your own subject matter objective and use it in the display.

Turn to a blank page in your notebook. On the first line write "Title: A Subject Matter Display of the Painting *Big Ben* by Andre Derain." Skip a line and write "What appears to be the end-in-view of the painting *Big Ben*?" On the next line write the objective given above or enter your own objective.

Assignment 3—Observe the Activities in the Painting

Look for activities in the painting. When observing a scene, the action takes the form of noticing the existence of things or how things are connected. For example, if you are looking at a mountainside you could observe trees growing, birds flying, and a deer running. These are referred to as states of being. Such observations can also be made when viewing a painting. For example, a painting of the Golden Gate Bridge contains a state of being (an activity) in the form of a bridge crossing over water.

Skip a line on your notebook page and enter the heading "Activities." Now, look at (i.e., study) the painting. Find the states of being that exist within the painting. As you discover them, list them under the Activities heading.

Assignment 4—Consider the Possible Consequences of the *Big Ben* Painting

Skip a line on your notebook page and enter the following lines. Leave a few blank lines after the terms "positive" and "negative."

What possible consequences may be attributed to the *Big Ben* painting?

From the artist's (Derain's) perspective:

- Positive (if end-in-view is achieved):
- Negative (if end-in-view is achieved):
- Positive (if end-in-view is not achieved):
- Negative (if end-in-view is not achieved):

From the viewer's perspective:

- Positive:
- Negative:

Now, consider the consequences of the *Big Ben* painting. For example, from Derain's viewpoint, a positive consequence of achieving his intent is that he spent time in a rewarding fashion. A negative consequence of not achieving his intent is a waste of time and materials.

Assignment 5—Write a Narrative on the *Big Ben* Painting

Your notes should now contain a three-stage MG2 subject matter display. The display elements represent a critical view of the topic. Use the display as an outline and write a narrative on the *Big Ben* painting. The narrative does not have to follow the order of the display. You are free to discuss the subject matter elements in any order you wish. In addition, if in your visits to the Internet you discovered more information about the painting or the artist, include it in your narrative.

Assignment 6—Develop a Subject Matter Display for Another Painting

Locate another painting or photograph. The painting or photograph can be located anywhere, on a wall in a building, in a book, on the Internet, or in your room. Develop a three-stage MG1 subject matter display for the item you select.

Teacher Resources

1. Fauve paintings in the style of *Big Ben* were first exhibited around 1905. They were denounced as amateurish and childlike in their bold use of color and dabbed brushstrokes. However, there were forerunners to the fauve style, such as Gauguin. "Color, Gauguin seemed to say, was as one felt it to be, not as it actually was" (Russel, 1969, p. 50). Van Gogh said, "I use color in a completely arbitrary way in order to express myself powerfully" (Russel, 1969, p. 62).

   When it debuted in 1905, the *Big Ben* painting was considered unrefined. One critic said it looked like "the barbaric and naive sport of a child who plays with the box of colors he got for a Christmas present" (Russel, 1969, p. 60).
2. For Assignments 3 and 4, consider placing students in groups.
3. Note the objective in the Figure 5.3 display. This is an instance where it is difficult to distinguish the intent of an originator from that of the subject matter being depicted. Nevertheless, by developing a subject matter objective based on what one sees or infers, one is still able to engage the subject matter critically using mind

Figure 5.3

Title: A Three-Stage MG2 Subject Matter Display on
Andre Derain's Painting *Big Ben*

(1) **What appears to be the purpose of the painting *Big Ben*?**
o The end-in-view of the painting *Big Ben* appears to be to depict the Big Ben clock tower and its surroundings in London, England.

(2) **Describe the activities that appear in the painting**
o Big Ben clock (presumably) keeping time
o sun setting [or rising]
o light glowing
o a river flowing
o water lapping
o a bridge crossing
o night coming (falling) or day dawning

(3) **What possible consequences may be attributed to the *Big Ben* painting?**
From Artist's Viewpoint

Positive (if purpose is achieved): Time spent in a rewarding fashion. Satisfaction in creating a new work of art. Possible acclaim.

Negative (if purpose achieved): Possible rejection of painting by critics / public. If the painting represented a new technique, by contemporary standards it might be considered an unsophisticated painting method and therefore not deserving of attention.

Positive (if purpose is not achieved): Artist gains experience. New knowledge of what not to do when painting. Basis established for trying anew.

Negative (if purpose is not achieved): No completed work-of-art to show for time spent. Frustration in not being able to achieve the desired effect. Waste of materials.

From Viewer's perspective:

Positive: Time spent viewing the painting is rewarded. Pleasure is achieved. Information is gained.

Negative: Little enjoyment of painting. Rejection of artist's work.

grammar strategy. If others disagree with an objective, they are free to develop their own subject matter display using their own objective.

4. The subject matter display shown in Figure 5.3 may be distributed to students (hard copy, screen projection, or digitally) after students have completed Assignments 1 through 5.

   Avoid suggesting that Figure 5.3 represents the only correct answer to Assignments 1 through 5. Variations are acceptable as long as they are consistent with what is shown in the *Big Ben* painting and with the proper application of mind grammar.

MUSIC

Assignment 1—Correct a Subject Matter Display

Figure 5.4 contains a two-stage MG1 subject matter display on music. Write the title and objective in your notebook. The activities are not in logical order. Place the list in logical order and write the corrected list in your notebook.

Figure 5.4

Title: A Two-Stage MG1 Subject Matter Display of Music

(1) **What is the meaning of music?**
  o Music has meaning because it represents the expression, projection, and reception of ideas and inner feelings.

(2) **What are the main activities associated with music?**
  o audience is engaged in music
  o artist is inspired to compose a piece of music
  o artist uses the elements of music (melody, harmony, rhythm, tempo, dynamics, timbre, and lyrics).
  o audience reacts on a variety of emotional and psychological levels
  o musicians learn to play the composition
  o audience attends performance or otherwise listens

Assignment 2—Identify Resources

Identify the resources mentioned in the list of activities you organized in Assignment 1. Write the response in your notebook.

Assignment 3—Write a Narrative

Write a narrative based on using the subject matter objective shown in the display, your corrected list of activities, and resources you identified.

Assignment 4—Think of Some Consequences of Music

From the audience's viewpoint, think of two positive and two negative consequences of music. Write them in your notebook.

Assignment 5—Listen to Music

We will now listen to a musical piece. At the end of the selection, think of one positive and one negative consequence. Think of examples in the music that illustrate each consequence.

Assignment 6—Develop a Music Pathway

Select an item in Figure 5.4 and develop a four-stage MG2 subject matter display for that item.

Teacher Resources

1. Figure 5.5 contains a subject matter display on music. This display may be distributed to students after assignments have been completed.

Figure 5.5

Title: A Four-Stage MG2 Subject Matter Display of Music

(1) **What is the meaning of music?**
o Music has meaning because it represents the expression, projection, and reception, of ideas and inner feelings.

(2) **What are the main activities associated with music?**
o artist is inspired to compose a piece of music
o artist uses the elements of music (melody, harmony, rhythm, tempo, dynamics, timbre, and lyrics).
o musicians learn to play the composition
o audience attends performance or otherwise listens via recordings.
o audience is engaged in music
o audience reacts on a variety of physical, emotional, and psychological levels

(3) **What are the consequences of music if its meaning is fulfilled?**
Positive: From the audience's viewpoint, music can result in (1) entertainment, relaxation, and vicarious experiences, (2) an aesthetic experience, 3) an ennobling, enriching, and deepening of one's nature, spirit, and emotions, (4) a better understanding of other cultures, and (5) a higher level of emotional maturity that enriches society and the quality of life.
Negative: From the audience's viewpoint, some music may (1) motivate audience to undesirable behavior, and (2) manipulate audience to a self-serving, pre-determined end.

(4) **Resource Bank** (persons, places, things, and ideas)

o composer	o musicians
o inspiration	o instruments
o elements of music	o audience

Vocabulary Box:
music: The art of arranging sounds in time so as to produce a continuous, cohesive, and suggestive composition through the elements of melody, harmony, rhythm, tempo, dynamics, and timbre.
melody: Melody is the arrangement of sounds that form a musical thought. It is like a sentence or phrase created not by words but by sounds.
harmony: The simultaneous sounding of different tones or notes.
rhythm: A pattern of notes of differing duration and stress. Rhythm can follow regular or irregular patterns and can cause one to engage in movement.
timbre: The characteristic tone of an instrument or a singing voice.
tempo: The speed and changes in speed felt during a piece of music.
dynamics: The volume and changes in volume heard during a piece of music.

2. Consider a homework assignment where students develop four-stage MG2 subject matter displays from (a) the composer's viewpoint and (b) the musicians' viewpoint.
3. Consider a homework assignment where students develop a subject matter display for a piece of music they select.

LISTEN TO A POEM

Assignment 1—Locate the Poem "Trees"

Follow the steps shown below and locate the poem "Trees," written in 1913 by Joyce Kilmer, an American poet. Then proceed to Assignment 2.

1. Visit https://librivox.org/.
2. Key in "Joyce Kilmer."
3. When the web page changes, click on "Joyce Kilmer (1886-1918)."
4. When the web page changes, scroll down the page and click on "Trees and Other Poems."
5. When the web page changes, scroll down the page and click on the little arrowhead above the section number 01.

Assignment 2—Listen to the Poem

Listen to the short poem "Trees," by Joyce Kilmer. It begins with the words "I think that I shall never see." You may listen to it several times before answering the following questions. Write your answers in your notebook.

1. What do you consider to be the end-in-view of the poem?
2. What activities are mentioned in the poem?
3. What are some possible consequences of the poem?

Teacher Resources

1. To introduce this instructional set, say something along the following lines to the class:

   > With practice, you can learn to apply mind grammar without having to develop a written subject matter display. You can read or listen to material and follow the discussion by looking for the elements of mind grammar. You can do this when listening to a lecture, an audiotape, a television debate, or spoken material in any form.

2. For additional information, see the instructional set Critical Visualization, in Chapter 4.
3. For additional listening material, visit the website given in this reference: Kilmer, J. (1913). *Trees and Other Poems*. Librivox—Free Public Domain Audiobooks. Retrieved from https://librivox.org/trees-and-other-poems-by-joyce-kilmer/.

THE BATTLE OF GETTYSBURG

Assignment 1: Critical Reading and Thinking

Part A: Table 5.3 contains a subject matter display in the form of a scrambled list. Use the space provided in column 1 and mark each item in the list as either subject matter objective (O), activity (A), positive consequence (C+), negative consequence (C–), or resource (R).

Table 5.3. The Battle of Gettysburg from the North's Point of View

O, A, C+, C–, or R?	**Title:** *A Subject Matter Display of the Battle of Gettysburg from the North's Point of View*
	Union forces inflicted casualties on the rebels (Southern forces) from which they would never recover.
	The purpose of the Battle of Gettysburg was to stop the Confederate army from continuing its invasion of the North in 1863.
	battlefield
	Southern forces move into Pennsylvania
	possible capture of Washington, DC
	soldiers
	Southern forces move toward Harrisburg, PA
	weapons
	Northern forces follow Confederate forces
	horses
	Union forces stopped the Confederate forces from being in a position to attack Washington, DC
	Southerners look for shoes in Gettysburg
	officers
	Northern armies could have been destroyed
	soldiers from both sides meet on the outskirts of town
	maps
	the battle is joined
	supplies
	fighting continues for three days
	Northern forces win the battle
	Union forces (the North) stopped the Confederate forces (the South, the rebels) from continuing the invasion.
	the Confederate invasion would continue

Part B: Work by yourself. Produce a subject matter display based on the marked list of items developed in Part A. Write the display in your notebook.

Assignment 2—Critical Listening

Use the battlefield maps given in class to follow the discussion as the teacher describes how the battle unfolded when the North and South forces took up their field positions. Write down at least three resources and three activities described by your teacher. Now, look at the display in your notebook. If the elements you wrote down are not in your display, add them to your display.

Assignment 3—Critical Writing

Work by yourself and write a narrative using your subject matter display as a guide. Write the narrative in your notebook. Keep in mind that your narrative does not have to follow the order that the material appears in the display. Your narrative can follow any order. In addition, when writing, you can add other related facts and ideas.

Assignment 4—Critical Thinking: Another Viewpoint

Form groups of three. The subject matter display you developed in Assignment 2 takes the Union's point of view. Let us now develop a display from the Confederation's point of view. For this display, consider only the subject matter objective and the consequences.

Teacher Resources

The subject matter display on the Battle of Gettysburg shown in Figure 5.6 may be distributed to students after assignments have been completed.

Figure 5.6

Title: A Four-Stage MG2 Subject Matter Display of the Battle of Gettysburg from the North's Point of View

(1) **Purpose of the Battle (Why was the battle fought?)**
o The purpose of the battle of Gettysburg was to stop the Confederate army from continuing its invasion of the North in 1863

(2) **Activities Associated with the Battle (What happened?)**
o Southern forces move into Pennsylvania
o Southern forces move towards Harrisburg, PA.
o Northern forces follow Confederate forces
o Southerners look for shoes in Gettysburg
o soldiers from both sides meet on the outskirts of town
o the battle is joined
o fighting continues for three days
o Northern forces win the battle

(3) **Consequences of the Battle**
Positive: (1) Union forces (the North) stopped the Confederate forces (the South, the rebels) from continuing the invasion. (2) Union forces stopped the Confederate forces from being in a position to attack Washington, DC. (3) Union forces inflicted casualties on the rebels from which they would never recover.

Negative (If battle was lost): (1) The Confederate invasion would continue. (2) Northern armies could have been destroyed. (3) Washington, D.C. might have been captured.

(4) **Resources** (What resources were used to fight the battle?)
o battlefield
o maps
o soldiers
o horses
o officers
o supplies
o weapons

Vocabulary Box
o Union Army: the soldiers of the northern states
o Confederate Army: the soldiers of the southern states
o Invasion: militarily, an invasion is to try forcefully to take over an opponent's territory.

LINCOLN'S GETTYSBURG ADDRESS IN ENGLISH

Assignment 1—Find the Resources (Find the Nouns)

Text Box 5.1 contains Lincoln's Gettysburg Address. Read the Address and circle at least ten resources (people, places, things, or ideas). Work with a partner.

Text Box 5.1

LINCOLN'S GETTYSBURG ADDRESS

November 19, 1863

Fourscore and seven years ago our fathers brought forth on this continent a new nation, conceived in liberty, and dedicated to the proposition that all men are created equal.

Now we are engaged in a great civil war, testing whether that nation, or any nation so conceived and so dedicated, can long endure. We are met on a great battlefield of that war. We have come to dedicate a portion of that field as a final resting-place for those who here gave their lives that the nation might live. It is altogether fitting and proper that we should do this.

But, in a larger sense, we cannot dedicate—we cannot consecrate—we cannot hallow—this ground. The brave men, living and dead, who struggled here have consecrated it, far above our poor power to add or detract. The world will little note, nor long remember, what we say here, but it can never forget what they did here. It is for us the living, rather, to be dedicated here to the unfinished work which they who fought here have thus far so nobly advanced. It is rather for us to be here dedicated to the great task remaining before us—that from these honored dead we take increased devotion to that cause for which they gave the last full measure of devotion—that we here highly resolve that these dead shall not have died in vain—that this nation, under God, shall have a new birth of freedom and that government of the people, by the people, for the people, shall not perish from the earth.

Assignment 2—Find the Activities (Find the Verbs)

Read and underline all the activities (phrases or sentences that contain verbs) in Lincoln's Gettysburg Address.

Assignment 3—Identify the Intent (the Objective) of Lincoln's Gettysburg Address

Read the Address again. Also, look over the resources and activities you developed in Assignments 1 and 2. What do you think is the main purpose (i.e., the objective) of the Address? Write a complete sentence. Here are some ways to start the sentence: (1) Lincoln's Gettysburg Address is important because . . . , (2) The end-in-view of Lincoln's Gettysburg Address is to . . . , and (3) Lincoln's Gettysburg Address has meaning because. . . . Select one of these approaches, or develop your own approach. Write your subject matter objective in your notebook.

Assignment 4—Develop a Three-Stage MG1 Subject Matter Display

Based on Assignments 1, 2, and 3, develop a three-stage MG1 subject matter display. Write the display in your notebook. Make sure the display has a title.

Assignment 5—Identify the Consequences within the Address

Find the consequences within the Address. Then update your MG1 display to an MG2 display by adding the consequences.

Assignment 6—Translate Your MG2 Display into Another Language

Translate your MG2 subject matter display into a language you have studied or know, or a language you are now studying.

Teacher Resources

1. The reference for Lincoln's Gettysburg Address in English is *The Citizen's Almanac* (2014). U.S. Department of Homeland Security, Washington, DC, 2014, p. 33.
2. The subject matter display shown in Figure 5.7 contains material that represents answers to both Assignments 4 and 5. It may be distributed to students after assignments have been completed. For more on Figure 5.7, see item 3 below.
3. The display in Figure 5.7 does not represent a single correct interpretation of the Address. Although there should be little disagreement on the activities and resources, the objective and consequences of the Address are open to interpretation. See How to Tell If a Display Based on Rhetoric-Loaded Material Is Acceptable, under the heading Additional Teacher Resources, in Chapter 4.
4. For a Spanish-language version of Figure 5.7, see Figure 4.5.
5. For a Spanish-language version of this instructional set, see Lincoln's Gettysburg Address in Spanish in Chapter 4.

Figure 5.7

Title: A Four-Stage MG2 Subject Matter Display of Lincoln's Gettysburg Address of 1863

(1) **What Was the End-in-View of Lincoln's Gettysburg Address?**

o The end-in-view of Lincoln's Gettysburg Address is to show that the soldiers at the battle of Gettysburg did not die in vain.

(2) **What Activities Are Described in the Gettysburg Address**?

o new nation brought forth 87 years ago
o now engaged in great civil war
o testing nation's endurance
o meeting to dedicate a burial ground
o field already dedicated by brave men
o instead, must have increased devotion to cause
o must resolve that man did not die in vain

(3) **Consequences**

The soldier's sacrifices would lead to a new birth of freedom; and that government of, by, and for the people shall not perish from the earth.

(4) Resources (persons, places, things, and ideas mentioned in the Address)

o years	o continent	o liberty	o devotion
o fathers	o civil war	o task	o lives
o new nation	o battlefield	o honored dead	
o men (brave, living, dead, honored)	o final resting-place	o God	
o people (us)	o ground	o freedom	
o beliefs (all men are created equal)	o world	o earth	
o government of, by, and for the people			

ADDITIONAL TEACHER RESOURCES

Here are several subject matter displays on a variety of topics. They may be used as the basis for designing classroom assignments and assembling them into an instructional set. Use them to design classroom assignments by pairing them, as you see fit, with the instructional techniques discussed in Chapter 3.

A Subject Matter Display of Perspective in Drawing

Figure 5.8

Title: A Four-Stage MG2 Subject Matter Display of Perspective in Drawing

(1) **What is the purpose of Perspective in Drawing?**

o The purpose of perspective in drawing is to represent a three-dimensional object on a two-dimensional surface.

(2) **How is a Three-dimensional Representation Made?**

o Select an object to represent in three dimensions [e.g., a shipping carton].
o Place a blank sheet of paper lengthwise in front of you on a table
o Draw a horizontal line across the sheet 1/3 down from the top of the sheet. The line is called a horizon.
o Place a mark *on* the right side of the horizon line. Place the mark a few inches from the center of the line. The mark is called a vanishing point [VP].
o With a straight edge, draw a 1.5" square a few inches below the horizon on the left side of the sheet.
o Lightly draw a line from each corner of the square to the VP. You should have four vanishing lines stretching to the VP.
o Mark a point two inches along the upper left vanishing line. Draw a horizontal line from this point to the upper right vanishing line.

o At the point where the horizontal line meets the upper right vanishing line, draw a vertical line until it touches the lower right vanishing line.
o The two lines you have just drawn represent the back end of the carton
o Erase all the vanishing lines from the back end of the carton to the VP
o Erase all the lines inside the carton.
o You now have a shipping carton represented in 3D [length, width, and height] on a 2D surface [the sheet of paper].

(3) **What are the Consequences of Developing 3D Drawing Perspectives?**
Positive: Objects can be made to look real. Artists can prepare a realistic sketch of what they want to paint. Illustrators can prepare vivid representations. Rendering in perspective improves a drawing because it better promotes understanding.
Negative: Drawing in perspective can be difficult and time-consuming. If rendered improperly an object can be distorted.

(4) **Resources Bank** (What places, persons, and things are needed to develop three-dimensional drawings?)	
o an object to represent in 3D	o an artist or illustrator
o drawing materials	o a vanishing point
o blank sheet of paper	o a horizon line

A Subject Matter Display of Philosophy

Figure 5.9

Title: A Four-Stage MG2 Subject Matter Display of Philosophy

(1) **The Intent of Philosophy**
o The intent of philosophy is to find what more there is to life, nature, science, and economic, political, and social arrangements than is not already known.

(2) **The Process of Philosophy**
A natural human activity that through critical and creative thinking:

o attempts to explain the human condition
o challenges assumptions and concepts
o wrestles with the boundaries of current thought
o takes up questions that people generally don't agree on and "... where none of the suggested answers command widespread acceptance ..." (Stokes, 2008, p. 6)
o determines what to do with scientific discoveries regarding self, society, and the environment

(3) **The Consequences of Philosophy**
Positive
o Expands the boundaries of current thought
o Produces new perspectives on difficult problems
o Makes scientific discoveries
Negative
o Little unity in method, not a science, not an art. General lack of consensus regarding the method of philosophical inquiry, except that it includes the use of all three modes of critical thinking (1. Gaining understanding and comprehension, explaining; 2. Argumentation, and 3. Problem Solving), as well as creative thinking.
o Can be general lack of consensus regarding results (i.e., the conclusions reached through reasoning).

(4) **Resources** (persons, places, things, and ideas)	
o thinkers	o a topic of interest
o skill in thinking strategies (recall, logical, critical, and creative)	
o thinker's current day's context	
o shared assumptions and agreements regarding certain concepts	
o the thoughts of current and previous philosophers	

APPLICATION ASSIGNMENTS

The assignments below call for the design of instructional sets. Develop a four-stage MG2 subject matter display (or its mind grammar equivalent) as the basis for designing the set's classroom assignments. When designing the classroom assignments within a set, (1) select or adapt the instructional techniques from those given in Chapter 3, or create your own original instructional techniques; (2) include at least three assignments in each set; and (3) engage students in some combination of thinking, reading/speaking, writing/listening, and observing for critical understanding and/or comprehension using the MG1 and/or MG2 reasoning strategy of your choice.

1. [Art 1]

Using the instructional set The Painting *Big Ben* by Andre Derain as a guide, develop an instructional set on a painting that you select. You can use https://www.gallery-worldwide.com as a resource for locating works of art.

2. [Art 2]

Develop an instructional set based on Figure 5.8 on perspective in drawing.

3. [Music]

Develop a subject matter display for any entry you select from Figure 5.5 on music. Use the display to develop an instructional set. For help on this assignment, see the discussion of itechniques 73 and 74 on pathways and waves in Chapter 3.

4. [Philosophy]

As a way to introduce students to the topic of philosophy, develop an instructional set based on Figure 5.9 on philosophy.

5. [Moby Dick]

Turn to the fifth paragraph on the first page of Chapter 10 (A Bosom Friend) in *Moby Dick* by Herman Melville. It begins "Whilst I was thus closely. . . ." Apply mind grammar to the paragraph and develop a three-stage MG2 subject matter display. Based on the display, develop an instructional set. As one of the assignments, have students develop another subject matter display based on another passage from *Moby Dick*. You can, of course, select another work of literature for this assignment.

The aim of all instructional sets is to actively engage students in new and revisited subject matter while concurrently developing their ability to think, read, listen, write, speak, and observe critically. Therefore, have in mind that the main aim of this instructional set on *Moby Dick* is to have students practice and gain competence in critical reading. It is not meant to suggest to you or your students that every paragraph or chapter in every work of literature must be engaged critically with mind grammar.

6. [Democracy]

Design an instructional set on the topic of democracy. The key to this set (or to any set), rests in the subject matter objective you develop for the subject matter display. For help on developing a proper subject matter objective, see the topic heading The Subject Matter Objective, in *Preparation for Critical Instruction: How to Explain Subject Matter While Teaching All Learners to Think, Read, and Write Critically* (Maiorana, 2016), page 44. When writing your subject matter objective, be sure not to include consequences.

7. [Law]

Develop an instructional set based on the general topic of, or a specific topic related to contract law, civil law, criminal law, or constitutional law. For help on identifying a specific topic, see the topic heading How to Develop a Topic for a Subject Matter Display, in *Preparation for Critical Instruction*, p. 59.

All the sample instructional sets in this book—as grade and discipline appropriate—can be used in primary- through college-level classrooms. This is also true of the instructional sets arising from the completion of end-of-chapter exercises. As do many of the classroom assignments within these instructional sets, exercise items 8 through 12 below lend themselves to group work in teacher preparation and professional development classrooms. In a given class, teacher-candidates or practicing teachers can be assembled into three groups, one each for capitalism, socialism, and communism.

Working as a group, group members develop one subject matter display and one instructional set for its topic as described in exercises 8 through 10. They then proceed to exercises 11 and 12.

8. [Capitalism]

Develop a four-stage subject matter display on the topic of capitalism. Be sure to write a proper subject matter objective (see Assignment 6). Do not include consequences in your subject matter objective. For help on developing consequences for the display, see Text Box 6.1, How to Develop Consequences, in *Preparation for Critical Instruction*, p. 78. Consider both short-term and long-term consequences.

9. [Socialism]

Develop a four-stage subject matter display on the topic of socialism. Be sure to write a proper subject matter objective (see Assignment 6). Do not include consequences in your subject matter objective. For help on developing consequences for the display, see Text Box 6.1, How to Develop Consequences, in *Preparation for Critical Instruction*, p. 78. Consider both short-term and long-term consequences.

10. [Communism]

Develop a four-stage subject matter display on the topic of communism. Be sure to write a proper subject matter objective (see Assignment 6). Do not include consequences in your subject matter objective. For help on developing consequences for the display, see Text Box 6.1, How to Develop Consequences, in *Preparation for Critical Instruction*, p. 78. Consider both short-term and long-term consequences.

11. [Deliver the Instructional Sets]

One at a time, each group, as team teachers, delivers its instructional set to the other two groups as students. During this time, students take notes so they may complete Table 2.1 in Chapter 2, Assignment Assessment Factors.

12. [Prepare Summary Assessment Report]

Teams meet to discuss the assessment reports they received on their instructional set from members of the other two groups. As a group, they again complete Table 2.1. This table summarizes all the comments they received from the other two groups. Each team member receives a copy of the summary table. Each team member then writes his or her own summary assessment report for his or her group's instructional set. The report is based on the completed summary table and whatever else the groups wish to include.[1]

NOTE

1. The tables, completed during or shortly after the delivery of the assignments, represent what are called "formative" reports. They are so called because they represent comments/evaluations made during the process of delivering (i.e., actively forming) the classroom assignments. The summary report is called a "summative" report. This is because such reports represent a summary of all the formative comments/evaluations.

BIBLIOGRAPHY

Art Gallery Worldwide (2009). The place to find your art. https://www.galleryworldwide.com

Derain, Andre. (1906). *Big Ben.* Retrieved from https://www.artsy.net/artwork/andre-derain-big-ben

Fauvism. Retrieved from http://www.metmuseum.org/toah/hd/fauv/hd_fauv.htm

Kilmer, Joyce (n.d.). Trees and other poems. Librivox. Retrieved from https://librivox.org/trees-and-other-poems-by-joyce-kilmer/

Maiorana, V. P. (2016). *Preparation for critical instruction: How to explain subject matter while teaching all learners to think, read, and write critically*. Lanham, MD: Rowman & Littlefield.

Melville, H. (1851). *Moby Dick or the Whale*. Retrieved from https://ebooks.adelaide.edu.au/m/melville/herman/m53m/

Russel, J. (1969). *The world of Matisse, 1869-1954.* New York: Time-Life Books.

Stokes, P. (2008). *Philosophy: 100 Essential Thinkers*. New York: Enchanted Lion Books.

U.S. Department of Homeland Security. (2014). Lincoln's Gettysburg Address. *The Citizen's Almanac*. Washington, DC.

Chapter Six

Instructional Sets for Mathematics, Science, Engineering, and Technology

Subject Matter Objective: The purpose of mind grammar–based instructional sets in mathematics, science, engineering, and technology is to actively engage students in new and revisited subject matter while simultaneously developing their ability to think, read, listen, write, speak, and observe critically.

Getting the answer to a math, science, engineering, or technology exam question has a short shelf life. Once the exam is over, the answer is of little lasting value. Will students be able to solve a similar but different problem outside the classroom and test environment?

When students leave the crystallized knowledge of the classroom they step into the world of work and society. This is a world where matters, conditions, and settings change fluidly. This is a world that increasingly requires one to think, read, and write critically. Mind grammar helps assure that whatever the environment, subject matter, or problem that students now and in their future may face, they will be able to think, read, and write of it critically.

Traditional discussions of mathematics, science, engineering, and technology topics focus mainly on procedure. The larger context in which a procedure exists is minimized because of reliance on serialism-based instruction.[1] Such discussions are mainly descriptive. Describing a topic is not the same as explaining a topic.[2] Describing a topic serially provides no inherent basis for critical thinking, reading, and writing. This results in students learning mainly to follow procedures in a mechanical or rote manner to arrive at a desired result.

Without critical context, students are left without true comprehension[3] of a topic itself. The larger framework of facts and ideas within which the procedure exists needs to be explored, connected, and integrated critically. Such critical learning is what mind grammar provides. Mind grammar critical reasoning patterns allow you to instruct critically so students learn to think, read, listen, write, speak, and observe critically. This is true for all the mathematics, science, engineering, and technology topics they study.[4]

This chapter illustrates how to design instructional sets on a variety of topics. Each set contains a number of classroom assignments and teacher resources. The resources contain guides for using the assignments in class and additional instructional materials.

Included in this chapter are instructional sets on the circle, percentages, probability, subscripted variables, geography, electrically charged clouds, an immunization experiment, Ohm's Law of electricity, and the cell phone. The chapter section Additional Teacher Resources contains subject matter displays or narratives on counting, the digestive system, the large intestine, litmus paper, ethical drugs, and the electrical batteries used on the Apollo Program's Lunar Module, the spaceship that landed men on the moon. These displays may be used to develop instructional sets.

Application Assignments appear at the end of the chapter.

THE CIRCLE

Assignment 1—The Shape of the Circle

The moon and the penny have round shapes. The outer edge of such shapes is called a circle. Identify three examples of where the round shape of a circle (a circular shape) occurs in nature. For example, if you throw a stone into a pond, the surrounding ripples in the water will take on the shape of a series of circles.

Assignment 2—Circles in Everyday Life

Identify where the shape of a circle appears in everyday things. For example, the surface shape of a hockey puck is in the form of a circle.

Assignment 3—Circle Vocabulary

Think of a flat surface, like the top of a table. Now, assume the shape of the table is round, like a circle. The distance all around the edge of the table/circle is called the circumference. Now, in your mind, place a penny at the center of the table/circle. The distance from the center of the penny to any point on the edge of the table/circle is called the radius. The distance of a straight line through the center of the penny from one edge of the table/circle to the opposite edge is called the diameter. The space that the round tabletop takes up is called the area. Draw a circle in your notebook. In your drawing, identify (show, mark) the circle's circumference, radius, diameter, and area.

Assignment 4—Calculate the Area of Your Circle

The Egyptians, Greeks, and Chinese discovered the ratio of a circle's circumference to its diameter as 3.14159 to 1. No matter how small or large the circle, the ratio value is always the same. It was decided to name the ratio after the sixteenth letter in the Greek alphabet. The sixteenth letter is called *pi* and here is its symbol: π.

The discovery of the value for pi (π) led to a series of formulas for the circle. These formulas can be used to calculate a circle's mathematical values. The formulas include area of a circle, $A = \pi r^2$, and circumference of a circle, $C = 2\pi r$ or $C = \pi d$. Let's assume that the circle in your notebook has a diameter of 3 inches. Calculate the distance around the circle (the circumference). Use 3.14 for the value of π.

Assignment 5—The Meaning of a Circle

Based on Assignments 1 through 4, write a complete sentence that represents an answer to this question: Why does the circle have meaning? You can also write the complete sentence by answering this question: Why is the circle important?

Teacher Resources

1. Assignment 5 addresses the circle's subject matter objective. Answers can vary widely and, given the preceding assignments, can all be valid. What you are looking for is (a) Is the subject matter objective valid in its use of mind grammar and (b) is the statement written in the form of a grammatically correct and complete sentence?
2. After Assignment 5, a sixth assignment using a three-stage MG1 version of Figure 6.1 may be used to introduce students to critical learning. A follow-up assignment can then be used to introduce the concept of consequences. At that point, Figure 6.1 can be made available to students.

Figure 6.1

Title: A Three-Stage MG2 Subject Matter Display of the Circle

(1) **Why Does the circle have meaning?**

o The circle has meaning because its physical shape provided the basis for early technology and an object of wonder.

(2) **What activities are associated with the circle?**

The Circle in Everyday Life and Art

o Wheels in the form of circles provided the basis for the potter's wheel, the water wheel, the cart and wagon wheel, and the spinning wheel.

o Huts, teepees, and igloos are built in the form of a circle.

o Pioneers formed circles with their wagons for safety

o Circles are used in artistic expression and in architecture

The Circle in Mathematical History

o Babylonians discovered the relationship between the circumference and diameter in a circle.

o The Bible mentions the ratio of a circle's circumference to its diameter as three to one.

o The Egyptians, Greeks, and Chinese discovered the ratio of a circle's circumference to its diameter as 3.14159 to 1. This value is represented by π (Pi), the 16th letter in the Greek alphabet.

(3) **What consequences are associated with the circle?**

Positive: Thousands of years ago, people wondered about the circle. This led to the discovery and application of the circle's mathematical properties.

Mathematical: The discovery of the value for Pi (π) led to a series of formulas used in mathematical calculations. The formulas include: Area of a circle: $A = \pi r^2$, Circumference of a circle: $C = 2\pi r$ or $C = \pi d$. Circle properties are also used to describe ideas and formulas in plane geometry and trigonometry.

Technological: The mathematical formulas associated with a circle make it possible to design and manufacture a variety of products including aircraft, automobiles, ball bearings, buildings, cameras, clocks, coins, computers, containers, cooling fans, electrical devices, furniture, gears, machinery, pulleys, radios, spacecraft, sports equipment, television sets, tires, and wheels.

Negative: Mathematical knowledge of the circle has led to the design of complex war weapons.

Vocabulary Box

Circle: A plane curve everywhere equidistant from a given fixed point, the center.

Planar: A flat surface

Area: The planar region bounded by a circle

Circumference: The distance around the boundary of a circle

Diameter: A straight line from one side of a circle to another side of that circle that passes through the center of that circle.

Radius: = The distance between the center of a circle and any point on its circumference.

PERCENTAGES

Assignment 1—Read a Narrative on Percentages and Develop a Subject Matter Display

Read the narrative on percentages in Text Box 6.1 and develop a three-stage MG1 subject matter display on calculating a percentage.

Text Box 6.1

PERCENTAGES

The function of a percentage is to show how often a part of the whole of something occurs.

Assume we have a group of 76 people. Thirty-two of them weigh less than 150 pounds. In this situation, the number 76 represents the whole of something (a group of people). The number 32 represents the share or part of the whole (the number of people under 150 pounds). Say we want to express, as a number, the share of people under 150 pounds as related to the whole number of people in the group.

Knowing the part or share of a whole is called knowing the percentage. In our case we want to know what part or share 32 is of 76. The word percentage is rooted in the Latin language. "Per" means accounting for the occurrence of something. "Cent" means one hundred. Putting per and cent together gives us the word percent or percentage.

Therefore, the word percentage means accounting for the occurrence of something in particular (e.g., people less than 150 pounds), every time it occurs based on a whole group of 100 somethings (people of various weights). Or, a percentage is how often something specific happens per one hundred somethings. Or, a percentage is a number that represents a part of a whole expressed in hundredths. The symbol for percent is %.

In calculating a percentage, the whole of the something is called the base value. The particular part or share of the something is called the value of interest. In our example, the base value is 76 and the value of interest is 32.

A percentage value is calculated as follows. (1) Identify the base value (76). (2) Specify a value of interest (32). (3) State the relationship as a ratio (32/76). (4) Convert the ratio to a decimal (32/76 = 0.42). (5) Convert the ratio into a percentage by multiplying by 100 ($0.42 \times 100 = 42$ percent, or 42%).

(6) We can now say the percentage of people who weigh less than 150 pounds in the group of 76 people is 42%. (7) Check to see if the answer is reasonable. The number 32 is less than half of 76. So we would expect the answer to be less than 50%. Therefore, the value 42% is reasonable.

Summary of above: A Percentage (%) Value = (The Value of Interest/Base Value) × 100.

Assignment 2—Apple Percentages

There are eighty-nine apples in a large basket. Fifty-seven of them are red, twenty-six are green, and six are spoiled. Calculate the percentage of red, green, and spoiled apples. Round your calculations to one decimal place.

Assignment 3—Create Another Calculation Example

Create a situation that has a base value of more than one hundred. Identify three values of interest. Then calculate the percentage for each value of interest. Round your calculation to the nearest whole number.

Assignment 4—The Consequences of Percentages

Consider the consequences related to percentages. For example, what might be the positive consequences of calculating a percentage value? In other words, in what ways can percentage values be used to promote clarity and understanding? What might be the negative consequences of calculating a percentage value? In other words, in what ways can percentage values be miscalculated? In what ways can they be misused? Write your answer in your notebook in the form of two paragraphs, one for positive and one for negative consequences.

Teacher Resources

1. Following is an answer for Assignment 4 on consequences. The positive consequences of percentages include their use in representing interest rates and test score achievement; the results of surveys that measure the popularity of people, ideas, and products; the relative amounts of ingredients in a package; and the growth or decline of stock values, body weight, and geographic populations.

   The negative consequences of percentages include their use in ways that are misleading. For example, assume a survey was conducted that measured the likeability of persons A and B. Person A had a likeability percentage of 75% and Person B, 25%. What if it turns out that one thousand people were asked about A and only four were asked about B? Is it fair, then, to accept the conclusion that A is three times more likeable than B? The answer is no. In this example, for the percentages to be comparable, the same people or nearly the same number of people should have been asked about both A and B.

2. The following can be used as a homework assignment. Write a narrative on percentages that includes only the subject matter objective and consequences.

PROBABILITY

Assignment 1—A Demonstration of Probability

Your teacher will provide you with a subject matter display on probability. Follow the discussion as your teacher leads the class through the display.

Assignment 2—Gaining Understanding

Describe why probability is important. Provide an example of probability from your own life. Write the answer in your notebook.

Assignment 3—A Bag of Jelly Beans

a. These jelly beans are in a bag: five yellow, four red, two blue, three green, one orange, and two pink. Let's say you close your eyes and pick a jelly bean from the bag.

   The most likely outcome is that you will pick a _________ jelly bean. The least likely outcome is that you will pick a __________ jelly bean. An impossible outcome is that you will pick a ______ jelly bean. You have an equal chance of picking a _____ jelly bean and a ______ jelly bean.

b. What is the probability of picking a yellow jelly bean? What is the probability of picking a pink jelly bean? To answer, follow the procedure given in the Assignment 1 subject matter display.

Assignment 4—Something Blue

The situation: Your best friend, Daria, has two blue sweaters, two red sweaters, one blue shirt, one blue skirt, two yellow blouses, four blue dresses, four blue slacks, two white blouses, and two blue scarves.

The question: What is the probability that Daria will wear something blue to school?

Assignment 5—A Spinner Board

The situation: A spinner board is needed. The board must be divided into eight equal sections. Each section must have a different color. The probability of landing on a green section is 3/8; on white, 0/8; on blue, 2/8; and on black, 1/8. The probability of landing on yellow and red must be equal.

The question: What would the spinner board look like? Lay out the spinner board design in your notebook. Instead of using color pencils, label each section by writing in the name of a color.

Teacher Resources

At the beginning of Assignment 1, distribute and discuss the probability display in Figure 6.2.

Figure 6.2

Title: A Four-Stage MG2 Subject Matter Display of Probability

(1) **Why is probability important?**
o Probability is important because it tells us the likelihood that a specific event will occur.

(2) **How is a probability figured out?**
1. Establish the situation
For example, a single coin will be tossed.
2. Identify the total number of possible outcomes
There are two possible outcomes; the coin will show either heads or tails.
3. Identify the outcome of interest
For example, assume "heads" is the outcome of interest.
4. Identify the number of times the outcome of interest can occur in the situation.
When a coin is tossed once, "heads" can show up only once.
5. Divide the number of times the outcome of interest can occur by the total number of possible outcomes: This gives us *1 / 2.*
6. State the probability.
There is one chance in two that a tossed coin will show heads. Or, there is a 50% chance that a tossed coin will show heads.

(3) **Consequences – How can we use the knowledge that a specific event is likely to occur?**
Positive use of probability knowledge: We can avoid taking a poor chance. For example, we know the most people who start smoking cannot stop smoking. Therefore, we will not start to smoke because the likelihood of stopping is too low and the likelihood of getting a serious illness is too high.

Negative use of probability knowledge: People can be cheated. A person who does not know the likelihood that something will happen can be taken advantage of. For example, the likelihood of winning money from a slot machine in a gambling casino is very low. If you don't know that this is the case, then you will lose your money.

(4) **Resources** – What is needed to figure out a probability?
o a probability situation o a desire or need to know that a specific event will occur.

SUBSCRIPTED VARIABLES

Assignment 1—Read a Narrative

Read the narrative in Text Box 6.2 on subscripted variables and develop a two-stage MG1 subject matter display. In the activities part of the display, replace the body weight example with one of your own.

Text Box 6.2

SUBSCRIPTED VARIABLES

A variable is something that changes or varies. "Sub" means below and "script" means write. So subscript means something written below, as in T_1. The letter T in T_1 represents the name of a variable (say, the daily temperature). The subscript 1 in T_1 represents the first in a series of temperature readings. Therefore, a subscripted variable (e.g., T_1, T_2, T_3, . . . T_N) is a way to represent a series of similar numeric values that change. Said another way, the purpose of a subscripted variable is to represent different numeric values (e.g., 60°, 72°, 85° centigrade) of the same variable (e.g., air temperature).

The resources needed are a physical quantity that changes and a symbol to name the quantity. Assume the physical quantity is body weight. Then (a) determine how many variables are needed (in this example, one, for body weight), (b) name the variable (for example, the letter W), (c) determine the number of variable values (e.g., 5), (d) assign subscripts to the variable (e.g., W_1, W_2, W_3, W_4, W_5), and (e) write an expression or formula that uses the subscripted variable. For example, if the quantities are to be added, the formula is Total $W = W_1 + W_2 + W_3 + W_4 + W_5$. A large number of values can be shown as Total $W = W_1 + W_2 + \ldots W_n$. The subscript n represents the name of a particular value or the representative name of the last value.

A positive consequence of using subscripted variables is that variables that contain more than 26 quantities (the number of letters in the alphabet) can be easily represented.

Assignment 2—Demonstration of the Use of Subscripted Variables

Follow the discussion as your teacher demonstrates how to solve this problem.

The situation: A company has seventy-two employees.

The challenge: Develop a formula to calculate the average pay of all employees.

Assignment 3—Solve a Subscripted Variable Problem

The situation: A company has 119 employees. Most employees earn a different hourly wage and work a different number of hours per week. Some employees work part-time (thirty-nine) and some a full forty-hour week (eighty). The payroll office must calculate the paycheck of each part-time and each full-time worker and then the total value of all paychecks.

The challenge: Develop three formulas: one to calculate each part-time employee's paycheck, one to calculate each full-time employee's paycheck, and another to calculate the total weekly payroll.

Assignment 4—Consider the Consequences

What are the positive and negative consequences for the employees and the company of solving the subscripted variable problem posed in Assignment 3?

Teacher Resources

1. For Assignment 1—Read a Narrative. This assignment is an example of how mind grammar for critical reading and thinking is seamlessly integrated into a math lesson.
2. For Assignment 2—Demonstration of the Use of Subscripted Variables. Here is a sample solution: (a) Determine how many variables are needed. There is one variable, the earnings of each employee. (b) Assign E as the name of the variable. (c) Determine the number of variable values (72). (d) Assign subscripts (E_1, E_2, . . . E_n). (e) Write a formula for average pay: Average Pay = ($E_1 + E_2 + \ldots E_{72}$)/72.
3. For Assignment 3—Solve a Subscripted Variable Problem. Here is a sample solution: (a) Determine how many variables are needed (two, one for part-time employees and another for full-time employees). (b) Name the variables (PT for part-time employees and FT for full-time employees. (c) Determine the number of variable values (PT = 39 and FT = 80). (d) Assign subscripts to the variable ($PT_1 \ldots PT_{39}$ and $FT_1 \ldots FT_{80}$. (e) Write three formulas that use the subscripted variables: (1) The formula for the pay of a part-time worker is PT_n = hours worked × hourly wage rate. (2) The formula for the pay of a full-time worker is FT_n = 40 × hourly wage rate. (3) The formula for the total weekly payroll is Total Pay = ($PT_1 + PT_2 \ldots PT_{39}$) + ($FT_1 + FT_2 \ldots FT_{80}$).
4. For Assignment 4—Consider the Consequences. Here are some consequences to consider. *Positive* (if the problem is solved using subscripted variables): The company will know how much money to deposit in the bank to cover the total weekly payroll. *Negative* (if the problem is not solved using subscripted variables): The formulas will not be available to process payroll data accurately and efficiently by computer. You and your students may think of others. The idea is to promote consequential thinking. Encourage responses. To the degree possible, be accepting of student responses. Even help them to modify their responses so they become acceptable.

GEOGRAPHY

Assignment 1—A Critical Look at Geography

Your teacher will distribute or otherwise direct you to a subject matter display on geography. Follow along as your teacher reviews this subject matter display with you.

Assignment 2—Write a Narrative on Geography

Write a narrative on geography. Use the subject matter display in Assignment 1 as a writing guide. Write the narrative in your notebook.

Assignment 3—Mercator and Gall-Peters Geographical Maps

Visit these websites: http://www.petersmap.com/page2.html and http://www.business insider.com/mercator-projection-v-gall-peters-projection-2013-12. Read the material and discover the difference between a Mercator projection map and a Gall-Peters projection map. Then in your own words, write a description of how the maps differ.

Assignment 4—Investigate Different Types of Theme-Based Maps

Visit this website: http://geography.about.com/od/understandmaps/a/map-types.htm. You will find descriptions of different types of thematic maps. Select one type of map and develop a three-stage MG1 subject matter display. Title the display A Subject Matter Display of a (enter theme type) Map. Write the display in your notebook.

Teacher Resources

1. In Assignment 1, after stating the purpose of geography, review the terms shown in the display. For example, you can tell students that "differentiate" means to show

Figure 6.3

Title: A Four-Stage MG2 Subject Matter Display of Geography

(1) **What is the Purpose of Geography?**
o A purpose of geography is to differentiate the areal features, characteristics, and use of the earth's surface.

(2) **What activities are associated with Geography?**
Research Geographic Data
o gather data on the elements of geography (physical features of land, use of land, populations, and industries)
o classify and organize the data
Turn Data into Information So Others May Understand
o describe areal features in words, pictures, maps, and representations
o describe land use, populations, and industries in words, tables, pictures, and graphs
Make Information Available to Others
o Prepare reports containing words, tables, pictures, and graphs
o Distribute reports
o update reports

(3) **What are the consequences of Geography?**
Positive (if the purpose of geography is achieved): Information on the earth's areal relationships is made available; ability to navigate great distances; ability to predict impact of proposed or anticipated economic, political, and military actions or events.
Negative (if the purpose of geography is not achieved): Ignorance of the physical and other features of the earth, potential danger and harm when exploring uncharted land and water.

(4) **Resources** (Persons, places, and things associated with geography)

o elevation	o topography	o climate
o soil	o vegetation	o population
o land use	o industries	o unit areas of states
o earth coordinates		

Vocabulary Box
Areal: the physical characteristics of an area (e.g., size, climate, mountains, bodies of water)
Differentiate: to show the difference concerning two or more persons, places, things, or ideas.

how something is different. Then show, for example, how a baseball field is different from a football field. Ask students to differentiate other objects.

2. Assignments 1 and 2 can be used to introduce students to critical learning. For Assignment 1, provide students with a three-stage MG1 version of Figure 6.3. Follow up Assignments 1 and 2 with an assignment that introduces the concept of consequences. At that point, Figure 6.3 can be made available to students.

ELECTRICALLY CHARGED CLOUDS

Assignment 1—Review a Two-Stage MG1 Subject Matter Display

MG stands for mind grammar. Mind grammar is a reasoning strategy for thinking critically. Mind grammar is also used to read, listen, write, speak, and observe critically. Shown here in Figure 6.4 is a two-stage MG1 subject matter display on electrically charged clouds. Review the display. The words in *italics* represent activities.

Figure 6.4

Title: A Two-Stage MG1 Subject Matter Display of Electrically Charged Clouds

(1) **Subject Matter Objective**
o An effect of electrically charged clouds can be a bolt of electricity (lightning).

(2) **What are the cloud activities that cause a bolt of electricity (lightning)?**
Buildup
o large amounts of electricity *accumulate* at the bottom of clouds
o the excess electricity *seeks* an escape route
Discharge
o the tallest thing in the area (e.g., a cell phone tower) *provides* an escape route
o a bolt of static electricity (lightning) *links* the cloud with another cloud or the tallest thing in the area

Assignment 2—Write a Narrative

In your notebook, write a narrative on electrically charged clouds. Use the subject matter display as a writing outline.

Assignment 3—Identify the Resources

A noun is a person, place, thing, or idea. In mind grammar reasoning strategy, nouns are called resources. In your notebook, list all the resources that appear in Figure 6.4. For example, "electrically charged clouds" is a resource.

Assignment 4—Think of Consequences

A consequence is what can happen after something else has taken place. Consequences go with everything in life. There are consequences that follow what you do or do not do. Consequences can be good (positive) or bad (negative). To be a critical thinker in life, consequences must be recognized, comprehended, and dealt with.

There are also consequences associated with all the subject matter topics you study. In your notebook, answer this question: What good and bad things can happen as a consequence of a bolt of lightning?

Teacher Resources

1. To further set up Assignment 4, provide students with a copy of How to Develop Consequences (see Text Box 6.1 on page 78) in *Preparation for Critical Instruction: How to Explain Subject Matter While Teaching All Learners to Think, Read, and Write Critically* (Maiorana, 2016b).
2. The subject matter display shown in Figure 6.5 may be handed out to students after all assignments have been completed.

Figure 6.5

Title: A Four-Stage MG2 Subject Matter Display of Electrically Charged Clouds

(1) **Subject Matter Objective**
o An effect of electrically charged clouds can be a bolt of electricity (lightning).

(2) **What are the cloud activities that cause a bolt of electricity (lightning)?**
Buildup
o large amounts of electricity *accumulate* at the bottom of clouds
o the excess electricity *seeks* an escape route
Discharge
o the tallest thing in the area (e.g., a cell phone tower) *provides* an escape route
o a bolt of static electricity (lightning) *links* the cloud with another cloud or the tallest thing in the area

(3) **Consequences of a lightning (electrical) discharge**
Positive: (1) Can inspire wonder. (2) Allowed Benjamin Franklin to prove that lightning and electricity are the same. (3) Led to the invention of the lightning rod (by Benjamin Franklin) for placement on buildings. (4) Knowledge of its potential for damage will lead people to avoid standing in an open area during a lightning storm.
Negative: (1) Injury and perhaps death if struck by lightning. (2) Can cause property damage. (3) Many wildfires are ignited by lightning.

(4) **Resources**	
o large amounts of electricity	o an escape route
o clouds	o a tall thing (i.e., cell phone tower)

AN IMMUNIZATION EXPERIMENT

Assignment 1—Read a True Story

Text Box 6.3 contains a true story of a doctor who conducted an experiment. He was trying to find a way to protect people against the deadly smallpox disease. As you read the story, apply your knowledge of mind grammar and read for critical understanding.

Text Box 6.3

AN IMMUNIZATION EXPERIMENT

A Doctor, a Boy, Milkmaids, Some Cows, and the Deadly Smallpox Disease

In the spring of 1796, Dr. Edward Jenner of Berkeley, England, visited a milk farm. He struck up a conversation with Tess, one of the milkmaids. He noticed that her face was clear of smallpox scars and congratulated her on having escaped the disease. She said she could not get smallpox disease. When he asked why, she replied along the lines of "I can't get smallpox disease because I've already had cowpox disease."

Tess had contracted cowpox disease from milking the sore udders of cows infected with cowpox. Such cowpox-induced protection from smallpox disease was well known on dairy farms. That chance conversation between the milkmaid and the doctor led to the worldwide elimination of the deadly smallpox disease. Here is how that came to be.

Dr. Jenner decided to conduct an experiment. The purpose of the experiment was to see if he could protect (immunize) James Phipps, an eight-year-old boy, from smallpox disease. To perform the experiment, Dr. Jenner needed the pus from the hands of a milkmaid with active cowpox pustules on her hands. He also needed instruments with which to scratch and implant the cowpox pus into the boy's arm. To complete his experiment, he needed a smallpox patient with active smallpox pustules.

The experiment involved a number of activities. First, the doctor located Sara Nelmes, a milkmaid whose hands were infected with cowpox. He then inoculated the boy in the arm with pus taken from Sara's cowpox pustules. The boy became ill with a mild case of cowpox. He recovered a few days later.

After six weeks, the boy was inoculated with pus taken from a smallpox patient. No smallpox disease occurred in the boy. Several months later, the boy was again inoculated with smallpox pus. Again, no smallpox disease occurred in the boy.

Dr. Jenner's experiment resulted in these positive consequences. First, vaccination was invented. Second, human species and their domestic animals gained the protection of immunization through vaccination. Third, because it was safer, vaccination with cowpox replaced inoculation with smallpox. Fourth, inoculation with smallpox pus became a crime. Fifth, in 1979, a group of international experts stated that the planet Earth was free of smallpox. In 1980, the World Health Organization endorsed their statement.

The experiment had these actual and potential negative consequences. The boy was intentionally made to become ill. He was most likely not aware of the danger to which he was exposed. Therefore, he was an unwitting participant. Dr. Jenner could not be certain of the outcome of his experiment; therefore, the boy could have died of smallpox disease.

So there you have it, the true story of how a doctor, a boy, milkmaids, and some cows rescued the world from smallpox disease.

Key terms

contagious: a disease or infection passed to another person through touching
cowpox: a mild contagious disease of the cow
immune: to not be affected by a disease
immunization: to protect a person or an animal from a disease
inoculate: to implant into a person or animal a germ or virus to provide protection against that very same germ or virus
pustule: a pimple filled with pus
smallpox: a deadly, contagious disease in humans
vaccine: a substance that is implanted into a person or animal to protect against a specific disease

Assignment 2—Develop a Three-Stage Read Subject Matter Display

Based on Assignment 1, develop a three-stage MG1 subject matter display.

Assignment 3—Expand Your Three-Stage Display to a Four-Stage Display

Read Text Box 6.3 again. Identify passages that address the positive and negative consequences of Dr. Jenner's experiment. Add the consequences to the display you developed in Assignment 2.

Teacher Resources

1. For answers to Assignments 2 and 3, see Figures 8.3 and 8.2 on page 107 and 105 in *Preparation for Critical Instruction.*
2. As a follow-up assignment (perhaps a term paper), consider having students identify and develop a four-stage subject matter display for another disease that medical science has overcome. Students then write an essay based on what they have discovered. For more on writing for critical explanation, see Chapter 8 in *Preparation for Critical Instruction.*

OHM'S LAW OF ELECTRICITY

Assignment 1—Read a Narrative

Read the narrative in Text Box 6.4 on Ohm's Law of electricity.

Text Box 6.4

OHM'S LAW OF ELECTRICITY

A simple electrical circuit includes a lightbulb, a switch, and an electrical storage battery, all connected with electrical wire. However, to design and assemble such a circuit, three values must be established. These are the voltage of the battery, the current flowing through the circuit, and the resistance of the bulb and connecting wire.

Battery voltage represents the force or pressure applied to the circuit and is expressed in volts. Current represents the flow of electrons through the circuit and is expressed in amperes. Resistance represents the opposition to current flow in a circuit and is expressed in ohms using the symbol Ω. Assuming the temperature remains the same, resistance is the ratio between voltage and amperes, or $R = V/I$. This ratio is called Ohm's Law.

The function of Ohm's Law is to show the mathematical relationship among current, voltage, and resistance in an electrical circuit. The positive consequences of using Ohm's Law properly include the following: (a) One can calculate the current, voltage, or resistance in an electrical circuit when any two of the three variables are known. (b) Circuit components (e.g., switch size, wire size, and battery voltage and size) can be correctly sized and selected. (c) Circuit values can be determined without the need for actual measurements. (d) Readings of a resistance meter can be verified through calculation. (e) The law is adapted to calculate related electrical properties. For example, power consumed in watts is defined in terms of Ohm's Law as $W = V \times I$ or $W = I^2 \times R$; energy consumed in watt-hours is defined as $E = V \times I \times H$. (f) Electrical appliances, machines, and devices can be safely designed and manufactured.

A negative consequence is that if unit conversion is not applied, an incorrect answer will be calculated. For example, say that voltage and resistance are given as volts and ohms, but the current is given in milliamperes. The milliamperes must first be converted into amperes before applying Ohm's Law.

Here is an example of the use of Ohm's Law: (1) Identify which variable circuit characteristic is to be found—voltage, current, or resistance. Assume that resistance is to be found and that $V = 220$ volts and $I = 10$ amperes. (2) Identify the appropriate form of Ohm's Law. When solving for resistance, the appropriate form of Ohm's law is $R = V/I$. (3) Substitute the two known values into the equation to solve for resistance: $R = V/I = 220/10 = 22\ \Omega$. These other variations of Ohm's Law may be used: $I = V/R$ and $V = I \times R$.

Assignment 2—Develop a Three-Stage MG1 Subject Matter Display

Use the information in Text Box 6.4 and develop a three-stage MG1 subject matter display.

Assignment 3—Apply Ohm's Law

For three different situations, calculate voltage, current, and resistance when two of the three variable values are known. For each situation, you will need to create values for the two known variables. For example, to calculate voltage, create values for current and resistance. Repeat for the calculation of current and resistance using new values for each situation.

Teacher Resources

For an example of how Ohm's Law is adapted for engineering design work, see Figure 6.13 on the design of electrical storage batteries for a spacecraft.

THE CELL PHONE

Assignment 1—How a Cell Phone Works

Your teacher will distribute a two-phase MG1 subject matter display on the cell phone. Follow along as the contents of the display are discussed.

Assignment 2—The Consequences of Using a Wireless Cell Phone

The main positive consequence of a cell phone is that people can leave home and carry with them the ability to make phone calls wirelessly. In addition, people can communicate wirelessly when mobile even though the geographic location of one or both speakers is changing constantly. As electronics grew smaller and computers more powerful, additional, nonphone functions were added into the cell phone device. This led to additional positive consequences. Therefore, the modern cell phone device now performs many other functions. Name six of them.

There are severe negative consequences related to cell phone use. Find out what they are and write an essay that discusses what you discovered.

Assignment 3—Satellite Phones

A cell phone system transmits voice signals wirelessly via land-based cell towers. Satellite phones transmit voice signals wirelessly via satellites that orbit the Earth. Research the topic of satellite phones. Use your research results and develop a two-stage MG1 subject matter display similar to the one discussed in Assignment 1.

Teacher Resources

1. Figure 6.6 can be used for Assignment 1. Consider making a sketch on the board to illustrate the activities described in the Figure 6.6 subject matter display.
2. To help students complete Assignment 2, provide them with the website locations given under negative consequences shown in Figure 6.7.
3. Figure 6.7 can be distributed to students after Assignment 2 is completed.

Figure 6.6

Title: A Two-Stage MG1 Subject Matter Display of the Cell Phone

(1) **What it the function of a cell phone?**
o The function of a cell phone is to allow spoken communication.

(2) **What activities are associated with cell phones?**
A Mobile Phone System is Set Up
o The geographic area within a city is divided up into a series of adjoining land areas (i.e., cells).
o Within each cell, a wireless phone signal transmission tower is erected. The tower is called a base station. It handles calls to and from cell phones. Although in different cells (land areas), phones that are connected to the wireless tower system can still communicate; hence the name cell phone.
o To keep track of a cell phone's geographic location within a city, the phone company operates a Mobile Telephone Switching Office (MTSO), which is housed in a building.
o Cell phones are programmed to store the following information:
- a unique serial number assigned to the phone (called an Electronic Serial Number—ESN)
- a unique telephone number that serves as the basis for a Mobile Identification Number (MIN)
- a unique code number called a system identification code (SID).
o User buys a cell phone and selects a phone company (called a carrier), to carry their conversations
Cell Phone is Turned on by User and the Following Takes Place automatically.
o Phone looks for its carrier by transmitting the carrier's SID.
o Phone receives SID from a carrier. If SIDs match, a connection is established and the phone can now be used to place or receive a call.
o The phone also sends a registration request to the carrier's MTSO so the carrier can keep track of the phone's geographic location. In this way, it knows which cell the phone is in when it wants to find and connect the phone to a caller.
User Receives a Call
o A phone call is placed to the cell phone's number.
o The carrier's MTSO determines which geographical cell the phone is in.
o The MTSO establishes a connection between the caller's cell phone and the user's cell phone.
o The user's phone cell rings and a two-way conversation can now take place.
o If the user is mobile (e.g., traveling in a car), the conversation is automatically tracked from one cell area to another (i.e., from one base station to another).

Key Terms:
o *regular phone or telephone:* a device that is connected to another phone via wires. It allows two people to speak to each other even though they are in different geographic locations.
o *cell phone:* a device that is connected to another cell phone wirelessly via cell towers. It allows two people to speak to each other even though one or both of them are constantly on the move from one geographic location to another.
o *cell:* a geographic area that can cover ten or more square miles.

Figure 6.7

The Consequences of Cell Phone Use

Positive:

1. People can leave home and carry with them the ability to make phone calls wirelessly. People can communicate wirelessly when mobile even though the geographic location of one or both speakers is changing constantly.
2. The first cell phones were large and performed only the phone call function. As electronics grew smaller, and computers more powerful, additional, non-phone functions, were added into the cell phone device. This gave rise to the modern cell phone which performs a variety of additional functions ranging from internet connections, email, and texting to the calculator, camera, compass, flashlight; and to specialized applications related to games, travel, navigation, and many other areas.

Negative:

1. Cell phones produce electromagnetic fields. According to the World Health Organization, the great use of cell phones among younger people means a longer lifetime of exposure. It is possible that current research on the use of cell phone for periods exceeding fifteen years may show a health impact. Reference: http://www.who.int/mediacentre/factsheets/fs193/en/.
2. Other health related issues concern negative impact on emotions, increased stress, illnesses via germs, chronic pain, and vision problems. Reference: http://www.medicaldaily.com/5-reasons-why-cellphones-are-bad-your-health-247624.
3. Driving a car while using a cell phone has and can lead to serious accidents and injury. Using a cell phone while driving increases the probability of a crash by over 400%. Reference: https://www.aaafoundation.org/sites/default/files/CellPhonesandDrivingReport.pdf.

ADDITIONAL TEACHER RESOURCES

Here are several subject matter displays on a variety of topics. They may be used as the basis for designing classroom assignments and assembling them into an instructional set. Use them to design classroom assignments by pairing them, as you see fit, with the instructional techniques discussed in Chapter 3.

A Subject Matter Display of Arithmetic Concepts in Counting (Compressed)

Figure 6.8

Title: A Four-Stage MG2 Subject Matter Display of Counting (Compressed)

(1) **What is the purpose of counting?** o The purpose of counting is to establish how much of something exists. (2) **How does counting proceed?** o gather or observe the items to be counted o start counting by assigning number one to the first item o continue to count each item one after another, from first to last o recognize that the number of the last item counted represents the total amount of items o count again to check the first result (3) **What are the consequences of counting?** If the Purpose is Achieved (if you know how much of something exists). *Positive:* Quantities can be established, agreements can be made, records can be kept, fair shares can be apportioned, progress can be measured. Burdens can be shared more equally. An appreciation for things that may exist in small quantities may be developed. *Neutral:* Numbers by themselves hold little value. A human being must attach meaning to numbers. *Negative:* Knowing how much of something another person has can lead to hard feelings. If the Purpose is Not Achieved (if you don't know how much of something exists) *Positive:* If quantities are unknown, may be moved to make plans to conserve and protect the number of items you do have. An understanding of scarcity and conservation. *Negative:* Quantities cannot be established, specific agreements cannot be made, accurate records cannot be kept, fair shares cannot be precisely determined, progress cannot be accurately measured. **(4) Resources (What is needed?)** o items to count o a need to know how many items there are o a system for counting.

A Subject Matter Display of the Human Digestive System (Compressed)

Figure 6.9

Title: A Four-Stage MG2 Subject Matter Display of the Human Digestive System (Compressed)

(1) **What is a function of the digestive system?** o A function of the digestive system is to extract nutrients from food. (2) **How does the digestive system work?** o food enters body through mouth o food is passed to stomach o food is mixed with gastric juices o food broken down (nutrients extracted) in small intestine o undigested food passes into large intestine o the large intestine reabsorbs water, absorbs vitamins, eliminates undigested / indigestible material **(3) What are some consequences of the digestive system?** *Positive:* body uses nutrients to maintain itself. *Negative:* the absence of nutrients can lead to body breakdown (4) **What resources does the digestive system use?** o food o mouth o pharynx (throat) o esophagus (gullet) o small intestine o large intestine o rectum o anus o related organs (salivary glands, liver, gall bladder, pancreas)

A Subject Matter Display of the Large Intestine

Figure 6.10

Title: A Three-Stage MG2 Subject Matter Display of the Large Intestine

(1) **What is a function of the Large Intestine?**
o A function of the large intestine is to absorb vitamin K.

(2) **How is the Large Intestine Used?**
o bacteria feed on undigested food material
o bacteria produce vitamins K and B
o vitamins are absorbed with water

(3) **Consequences associated with the Large Intestine?**
Positive (if function is carried out): blood can clot
Negative (if function is not carried out): blood will not clot

A Subject Matter Display of Litmus Paper

Figure 6.11

Title: A Four-Stage MG2 Subject Matter Display of Litmus Paper

(1) **What is the purpose of litmus paper?**
o The purpose of litmus paper is to find out whether a substance is an acid or a base.

(2) **How is Litmus Paper Used?**
o Place the jar of liquid in front of you on a table.
o Dip a piece of blue litmus paper and a piece of red litmus paper in the liquid.
o If the blue litmus paper turns red, identify the liquid as an acid.
o If the red litmus paper turns blue, identify the liquid as a base.
o If the blue litmus paper remains blue, and the red litmus paper remains red, identify the liquid as neutral.

(3) **What can result if a liquid is/is not identified as acid, base, or neutral?**
Positive (if identified): (1) Unknown liquids may be categorized as either acid, base, or neutral. (2) Acidic and basic substances may be properly utilized in foods, medications, and other elements (e.g., swimming pool water).
Negative (if not identified): (1) Liquids will remain unidentified as regards their acidic and basic properties, (2) Acidic and basic substances will not be able to be properly utilized in foods and medications. (3) Improper testing procedures can lead to liquids being misidentified.

(4) **What is needed to conduct a litmus test?**
o a need to determine if the liquid is an *acid* (e.g., citric, acetic, boric, etc.), or a *base* (e.g., household ammonia, milk of magnesia, etc.), or is *neutral* (e.g., water, oil, etc.)
o test tube rack o a test tube containing a liquid
o red litmus paper o blue litmus paper

Vocabulary Box:
Acid: A compound that produces hydrogen ions in solution, has a sour taste, and turns blue litmus paper red
Base: A compound that produces hydroxide ions in solution, has a bitter taste and a slippery feel, and turns red litmus paper blue.
Neutral: A compound that is neither an acid nor a base.
Indicator: A substance that changes color in the presence of other substances.
Litmus Paper: Paper that has special powder in it. The paper can then serve as an indicator of whether a substance is an acid, base, or neutral.

A Subject Matter Display of Ethical Drugs for Human Use

Figure 6.12

Title: A Four-Stage MG2 Subject Matter Display of Ethical Drugs for Human Use

(1) **Purpose**
o The purpose of an ethical drug is to reverse or alter the impact of a disease.

(2) **Activities Associated with Developing an Ethical Drug**
General Pharmacology Activities
Develop Molecule as Follows:
o Identify the disease and develop an idea for a molecule for its treatment or cure
o Replicate the disease state in test animals.
o Develop molecule, establish and administer screening dose, and test on animals
o If test results positive, perform toxicology activities
Basic Toxicology Activities
Test Molecule for Adverse Events in a Living Organism as Follows:
o Determine mutations. If negative, perform chromosomal aberration test (CAT) of active molecule.
o Observe results of CAT test. If no adverse reactions, perform needed additional toxicology tests
o Test molecule in human volunteers with and without the disease for efficacy and adverse events. If little or no adverse events, the molecule may be considered an unapproved drug candidate at this stage.
o If FDA approves drug, make drug available to medical profession to prescribe for patient use.
o Perform post-market surveillance for adverse reactions.

(3) **Consequences of Realizing the Purpose of an Ethical Drug**
Positive (If drug proves effective in use)
For Patient: Relief from or cure of disease. For Doctor: Another tool in armamentarium. For Drug Company: Material and psychological rewards that go with developing a successful drug. For Pets: May benefit from drugs developed for humans
Negative (if drug proves to produce unexpected adverse reactions)
For Patient: No relief from or cure of disease and potential physiological damage. For Doctor: No tool added to armamentarium. For Drug Company: Drug can be recalled, can be sued by patients, can suffer monetary loss and receive negative publicity. For Test Animals: Suffer physiological pain and loss of life.

(4) **Resources Needed to Develop an Ethical Drug**
o a disease o active molecule o drug companies o pharmacologists o toxicologists
o lab technicians o medical doctors o well-equipped laboratories
o drug companies' Animal Care and Use Committee o Federal Drug Administration
o test animals o human volunteers with and without disease o money o time

Vocabulary Box
Drug: a substance that affects one's physiological or psychological state.
Ethical Drug: A drug approved by regulatory authorities for use in humans for a specific disease.
Molecule: The smallest physical unit of a chemical element or substance.
Chromosomal Mutation: A change in nature, form, or quality in genes and chromosomes
Aberration: DNA genetic material that deviates from its normal state.
Armamentarium: The resources available to a medical doctor to treat patient illnesses.

Notes:
1. The development of a molecule can take 5–7 years, perhaps more.
2. The development of a molecule leading to a drug could take 10 years and over 95% fail.

A Subject Matter Display of the Apollo Program's Lunar Module Electrical Storage Batteries

Figure 6.13

Title: A Four-Stage MG2 Subject Matter Display of the Engineering Design for the Apollo Program's Lunar Module Electrical Storage Batteries

(1) **Purpose of the Engineering Design of the Lunar Module's Electrical Storage Batteries**
o The purpose of the engineering design for the Lunar Module's electrical storage batteries was to design batteries that would meet the electrical energy requirements of the spaceship.

(2) **Activities** (What engineering design activities took place?)
o timeline for the Lunar Module's (LM) earth-to-moon landing mission established.
o electrical load analysis revealed the electrical energy requirements (watts x hours) for the LM's mission.*
o study showed the LM needed two ascent stage and four descent stage batteries.
o silver-zinc (Ag-Zn) battery type chosen.** Physical location of batteries in LM spacecraft, structural mounting, and heat rejection requirements determined battery cell arrangement and case dimensions.
o batteries designed by Grumman Aerospace Corporation engineers, technical specifications written, and Eagle Picher Industries chosen competitively to manufacture the batteries.
o batteries ground tested in laboratories, on the LM ground Test Article - 1 (LTA-1), and flight tested on the LM 1 (Apollo 5) unmanned, earth orbit, mission.
o batteries installed on LM Vehicles 3 through 12 for manned Apollo missions 9 through 17. Apollo 9 orbited the earth. Apollo 10 orbited the moon. Apollo 11 was the first manned lunar landing. Apollo 17 was the sixth and last manned lunar landing.

(3) **Consequences of the Engineering Design of Lunar Module's Electrical Storage Batteries**
Positive:
(1) The engineering design resulted in storage batteries that were able to successfully power the LM's operating systems through all Apollo missions. (2) When the Apollo 13's Command Module lost its electrical power, the LM batteries served as its "lifeboat" thus helping to save the lives of the astronauts.***
Negative:
The following *did not happen*, but *If* the batteries were improperly sized, designed, manufactured, and tested, then (1) shorted cells could produce great amounts of heat, disrupting the thermal control system and/or causing structural damage, (2) cell seals could leak caustic electrolyte, which could damage vehicle equipment and present an explosion hazard.

(4) **Resources** (What was needed?)
o The goal, will, and national commitment to land men on the moon as expressed by President John F. Kennedy in a speech to a joint session of congress on May 25, 1961: "I believe that this nation should commit itself to achieving the goal, before this decade is out, of landing a man on the moon and returning him safely to earth." Reference: www.nasa.gov/vision/space/features/jfk_speech_text.html#.v1g_qgnzzfi.
o moon mission time line, LM vehicle equipment energy usage (E = V x I x Hours), electrical load analysis
o highly motivated electrical, mechanical, and test engineers; technicians; and office staff
o Grumman Aerospace Corporation: designed, manufactured, and tested the Lunar Module.
o Eagle-Picher Company: battery manufacturer o National Aeronautics and Space Administration
o time o money o Lunar Module ground test article LTA-1 and LM-1 flight test article
o Ascent and descent stage batteries for ground and flight testing

Information Box
- Lunar Module: The first true manned vehicle designed to operate in outer space.
- LM's Operating Systems: electrical power storage, distribution, and control; descent and ascent engines; reaction control; environmental control; life support; communications; guidance, navigation and control; instrumentation; lighting; and landing gear.
- Lunar Module 5 (the Apollo 11 mission), landed two men on the earth's moon on July 20, 1969. The astronauts (Neil Armstrong and Buzz Aldrin), explored the moon, left the moon using the LM's ascent stage, and then rendezvoused successfully with the moon-orbiting Command Module and its pilot (Michael Collins). All three astronauts returned to earth safely on July 24, 1969.

APPLICATION ASSIGNMENTS

The assignments below call for the design of instructional sets. Develop a four-stage MG2 subject matter display (or its mind grammar equivalent) as the basis for designing the set's classroom assignments. When designing the classroom assignments within a set, (1) select or adapt the instructional techniques from those given in Chapter 3, or create your own original instructional techniques; (2) include at least three assignments in each set; and (3) engage students in some combination of thinking, reading/speaking, writing/listening, and observing for critical understanding and/or comprehension using the MG1 and/or MG2 reasoning strategy of your choice.

Mathematics

1. [Arithmetic—Concepts in Counting]

Develop an instructional set based on Figure 6.8.

2. [Arithmetic—Addition]

Develop an instructional set for addition.

3. [Algebra]

Develop an instructional set for an algebra topic.

4. [Geometry]

Develop an instructional set for a geometry topic.

5. [Trigonometry]

Develop an instructional set for a trigonometry topic.

6. [Statistics 1]

Develop an instructional set for a topic in descriptive statistics

7. [Statistics 2]

Develop an instructional set for a topic in inferential statistics.

8. [Calculus]

Develop an instructional set for a topic in calculus.

Science

9. [The Planet Earth]

Develop an instructional set on the planet Earth from the viewpoint of its human inhabitants.

10. [Digestive System]

Develop an instructional set based on the subject matter display in Figure 6.9.

11. [Large Intestine]

Develop an instructional set based on the subject matter display in Figure 6.10.

12. [Litmus Paper]

Develop an instructional set based on the subject matter display in Figure 6.11.

13. [Chemistry]

Develop an instructional set based on a topic in chemistry.

14. [Earth Science]

Develop an instructional set based on a topic in Earth science.

15. [Biological Science]

Develop an instructional set based on a topic in biological science.

16. [Medical Science]

Develop an instructional set based on a topic in medical science.

17. [Pharmacology]

Develop an instructional set based on the subject matter display in Figure 6.12.

18. [Nuclear Science]

Develop an instructional set based on a topic in nuclear science.

Engineering

19. [Aerospace]

Develop an instructional set based on a topic in aerospace engineering.

20. [Civil]

Develop an instructional set based on a topic in civil engineering.

21. [Electrical]

Develop an instructional set based on a topic in electrical engineering.

22. [Electrical]

Develop an instructional set based on the subject matter display in Figure 6.13.

23. [Mechanical]

Develop an instructional set based on a topic in mechanical engineering.

24. [Computer]

Develop an instructional set based on a topic in computer engineering.

Technology

Two of the topics addressed in this section address the Internet and a computer website. Each of these topics lends itself to numerous objectives. Adopt a point of view (e.g., Internet as a source of news, a website for shopping). Then write your subject matter objective accordingly and develop a subject matter display. Use the display to develop an instructional set. In your consequences, be sure to address the need to be skeptical of anything you may read on the Internet or on a specific website.

25. [The Internet]

Develop an instructional set on the Internet.

26. [A Computer Website]

Develop an instructional set for a specific website.

27. [Automobile Lane Departure Warning System]

Develop an instructional set for the automobile lane departure warning system.

NOTES

1. Because it provides no critical reasoning pattern for subject matter engagement, serialism-based instruction induces rote learning and provides no basis for critical reading and writing. See discussion on instructional strategies in Chapter 1, Fundamentals of Critical Instruction and Learning. For a full discussion of the great limitations of serialism-based instruction, see Chapter 2, Instructional Practice Is Inherently Weak: The Hidden Story, in *Fixing Instruction: Resolving Major Issues With a Core Body of Knowledge for Critical Instruction* (Maiorana, 2016a).
2. See Chapter 1 for the meaning of the word "explain" in an instructional context.
3. See discussion of the terms "understanding," "comprehension," and "explanation" in Chapter 1, Fundamentals of Critical Instruction and Learning.
4. For a full discussion of the difference between logical (serial) thinking and critical thinking, see Chapter 3, Thinking: The First Language Art, in *Preparation for Critical Instruction* (Maiorana, 2016b)

BIBLIOGRAPHY

AAA Foundation for Traffic Safety. (2008). Cell phones and driving: Research update. Retrieved from https://www.aaafoundation.org/sites/default/files/CellPhonesandDrivingReport.pdf

About Education. (2016). Types of maps. Retrieved from http://geography.about.com/od/understandmaps/a/map-types.htm

Adapted Mind. (2016). Math. Retrieved from http://www.adaptedmind.com/

Borreli, L. (2013). 5 reasons why cell phones are bad for your health. Retrieved from http://www.medicaldaily.com/5-reasons-why-cellphones-are-bad-your-health 247624

Desowitz, R. S. (1988). *The thorn in the starfish: The immune system and how it works*. New York: Norton.

Gordon, R. (1993). *The alarming history of medicine*. New York: St. Martin's Griffin.

Jenner, E. (1808). Two cases of small-pox infection. Retrieved from http://www.ncbi.nlm.nih.gov/pmc/articles/PMC2128795/pdf/medcht00073-0301.pdf

Maiorana, V. P. (2016a). *Fixing instruction: Resolving major issues with a core body of knowledge for critical instruction*. Lanham, MD: Rowman & Littlefield.

Maiorana, V. P. (2016b). *Preparation for critical instruction: How to explain subject matter while teaching all learners to think, read, and write critically*. Lanham, MD: Rowman & Littlefield.

Marshall B., Tyson, J., and Layton, J. (2000). How cell phones work. Retrieved from http://electronics.howstuffworks.com/cell-phone.htm

Merriam-Webster's collegiate dictionary (11th ed.). (2007). Springfield, MA: Author.

NASA News. (2013). NASA—Excerpt from the "Special Message to the Congress on Urgent National Needs" by President John F. Kennedy, May 25, 1961. Retrieved from www.nasa.gov/vision/space/features/jfk_speech_text.html#.V1G_QGNZZFI

National Oceanic and Atmospheric Administration. (2010). Thunderstorms, tornadoes, lightning: Nature's most violent storms. Retrieved from http://www.nws.noaa.gov/om/severe weather/resources/ttl6-10.pdf

Sterbenz, C. (2013). The most popular map of the world is highly misleading. Retrieved from http://www.businessinsider.com/mercator-projection-v-gall-peters-projection-2013-12

The Peters Map and the Mercator Map. Retrieved from http://www.petersmap.com/page2.html

World Health Organization. (2016). Electromagnetic fields and public health: Mobile phones. Retrieved from http://www.who.int/mediacentre/factsheets/fs193/en/

Chapter Seven

Instructional Sets for the Social Sciences

Subject Matter Objective: The purpose of mind grammar–based instructional sets in the social sciences is to actively engage students in new and revisited subject matter while simultaneously developing their ability to think, read, listen, write, speak, and observe critically.

This chapter shows how to design instructional sets on a variety of topics for the social sciences. Each set contains a number of classroom assignments and teacher resources for use with the assignments.

Included in this chapter are instructional sets on The First Amendment to the Constitution of the United States, An Economic System, Economists, The Declaration of Independence, and credit information agencies. The chapter section Additional Teacher Resources contains subject matter displays on Bloom's Taxonomy of Educational Objectives—Book I Cognitive Domain, economics, Maslow's Theory of Human Needs, a typical American business, and Martin Luther King Jr.'s "I Have a Dream" Speech. These displays may be used to develop instructional sets.

Application Assignments appear at the end of the chapter.

THE FIRST AMENDMENT TO THE CONSTITUTION OF THE UNITED STATES

Assignment 1—Read the First Amendment for Critical Comprehension

Text Box 7.1 contains the First Amendment to the Constitution of the United States. Read it using the MG2 critical reading procedure.

Text Box 7.1

> **FIRST AMENDMENT TO THE CONSTITUTION OF THE UNITED STATES**
>
> Congress shall make no law respecting an establishment of religion, or prohibiting the free exercise thereof; or abridging the freedom of speech or of the press; or the right of the people peaceably to assemble, and to petition the Government for a redress of grievances.

Assignment 2—Develop an MG2 Subject Matter Display

Form groups of three. Based on the results of Assignment 1, develop a three-stage MG2 subject matter display. A three-stage MG2 display includes a subject matter objective, activities, and positive and negative consequences.

Assignment 3—Write Your Consequential Version of the First Amendment

Write a narrative based on the display you developed in Assignment 2. Work by yourself.

Assignment 4—Explore Another Amendment

Any amendment to the U.S. Constitution can be engaged through MG2 critical reading. Select any other amendment to the Constitution and repeat Assignments 1 through 3. Work by yourself.

Teacher Resources

1. The subject matter display shown in Figure 7.1 and the narrative that follows in Text Box 7.2 may be distributed to students (hard copy, screen projection, or digitally) after students have completed Assignments 1, 2, and 3. Avoid suggesting that this display and narrative represent the only correct answers to Assignments 2 and 3. Many variations (including alternate ways of showing/displaying the mind grammar elements) are possible. Variations are acceptable as long as they are consistent with the original textual material and with the proper application of mind grammar.
2. The narrative in Text Box 7.2 uses Figure 7.1 as a writing outline. However, narratives do not have to follow the order of a subject matter display. For more on writing for critical explanation, see Chapter 7, Write for Critical Explanation, in *Preparation for Critical Instruction* (Maiorana, 2016b).
3. Regarding Assignment 4, for a copy of the Constitution of the United States in the form of a PDF document, visit https://www.uscis.gov and enter search term for

Figure 7.1

Title: A Four-Stage MG2 Subject Matter Display of
The First Amendment to the Constitution of the United States

(1) Purpose of the First Amendment

o The purpose of the first amendment to the Constitution of the United States is to prohibit any laws that limit freedoms associated with religion, speech, the press, assembling, and petitioning.

(2) Activities (What activities appear in the first amendment?)

o Government shall make no law that establishes a religion
o Government shall not prohibit the free exercise of religion
o Government shall not prevent people from:
- speaking freely
- printing material freely
- peaceably assembling
- petitioning government to redress grievances

(3) Consequences (What are some consequences of the first amendment?):

Positive: New religions can be established and practiced without being restrained. Individuals and organizations can establish communication channels to discuss and publicize their views on any issue. New forms of expression and communication may be developed (e.g., the internet), without fear of interference. Ideas and thoughts can be made known through speech and print. People can assemble and petition to express their ideas.

Negative: People may try to impose their religious beliefs on others. Things may be said or printed that are hurtful. People and organizations may get into fights (physical and intellectual), when expressing themselves on an issue. People may assemble and petition even though their ideas and issues may generally be considered repugnant.

(4) Resources (What persons, places, things, or ideas are mentioned in the 1st Amendment?)

o congress	o law	o government	o religion
o speech	o press	o people	o grievances

Vocabulary Box
amendment: a change that corrects or revises
abridge: to reduce or cut short
redress: to set right or fix

Text Box 7.2

A NARRATIVE ON THE FIRST AMENDMENT

The purpose of the First Amendment to the Constitution of the United States is to prohibit laws that limit freedoms associated with religion, speech, the press, assembling, and petitioning

To this end, government shall make no law that establishes a religion or that prohibits the free exercise of religion. Furthermore, government shall not prevent people from speaking freely, printing material freely, peaceably assembling, or petitioning government to redress grievances.

The positive consequences of the First Amendment are that new religions can be established and practiced, ideas and thoughts can be made known through speech and print, and people can assemble and petition to express their ideas.

The negative consequences of the First Amendment are that people may try to impose their religious beliefs on others, things may be said or printed that are hurtful, and people may assemble and petition even though their ideas and issues may be considered offensive by others.

M-654. You can also Google M-654. The twenty-seven amendments to the Constitution are referred to as Articles and appear on pages 31 through 46 of the document.
4. For additional information concerning the First Amendment, visit the First Amendment Center at http://www.firstamendmentcenter.org.

AN ECONOMIC SYSTEM

Assignment 1—Some Elements of an Economic System

(a) Review these terms associated with an economic system. Have one partner say the term and then have the other partner give the description of the term. Alternate roles.

- *Economic system:* an operating system for production, distribution, and consumption of goods and services (for example, capitalism, socialism, or communism)
- *Standard of living:* the quantity and quality of goods and services available to individuals or society
- *Land:* natural resources and physical property
- *Labor:* human effort
- *Capital:* buildings, machinery, equipment, money
- *Management:* overall coordination of production efforts
- *Good:* a tangible item (e.g., a computer)
- *Service:* a process (e.g., a haircut)

(b) Table 7.1 contains some elements related to economics. Identify the mind grammar nature of the items listed below in Table 7.1. In the space provided, mark each item in the list as purpose (P), activity (A), positive consequence (C+) or negative consequence (C–), or resource (R). Check your answers against those of other group members and resolve any differences.

Table 7.1. Some Mind Grammar Elements of an Economic System

P, R, A, C+, or C–?	*Mind Grammar Elements*
	If an economic system succeeds, then individuals and society can produce and raise the standard of living.
	land, labor, capital, management
	government
	An economic system is important because it functions to produce, distribute, and consume goods and services.
	a good is manufactured or a service is developed
	consumers shop for goods and services
	If an economic system fails, then individuals and society will suffer and have a lower or poor standard of living.
	labor unions
	good is shipped or service is made available

Assignment 2—Connect and Integrate the Elements of an Economic System

In Assignment 1 you identified elements related to economics. Use the results of Assignment 1 to complete the blank lines in the display shown in Figure 7.2. Check your answers with a partner.

Figure 7.2

Title: A Four-Stage MG2 Subject Matter Display of an Economic System (Incomplete)

(1) **Why is an economic system important?**

o ____
____.

(2) **What are the activities associated with economics?**

o General Activities
- an economic system is established
- government oversees economic activity
- economic system interacts internationally

o Production Activities
- land, labor, capital, and management are used to establish production or service facilities
- ____

o Distribution Activities
- good or service is marketed
- ______________________________.

o Consumption Activities
- supply and demand determines the price of goods and services
- ______________________________

(3) **What are some consequences of economics?**

Positive consequences: ____
______________.

Negative consequences: ____
______________.

(4) **What persons, places, things, and ideas (resources) are associated with economics?**

o _______, _______, _______	o consumers, workers o _______
o _____________	o Money, banking, and financial system
o entrepreneurs / businesses	o ___________

Vocabulary Box

economic system: an operating system for production, distribution, and consumption (for example: capitalism, socialism, or communism)
standard of living: the quantity and quality of goods and services available to individuals or society.
land: natural resources and physical property, *Labor:* human effort, *Capital:* machinery, *Management:* overall coordination of production efforts
good: a tangible item (e.g. a tablet personal computer), *service:* a process (e.g. a haircut)

Assignment 3—Write a Narrative

Write a narrative based on parts 1 and 2 of the display you completed in Assignment 2.

Teacher Resources

1. This instructional set may be used to introduce students to critical learning.
2. The subject matter display shown in Figure 7.3 may be distributed to students (hard copy, screen projection, or digitally) after students have completed Assignments 1 and 2.

Figure 7.3

Title: A Four-Stage MG2 Subject Matter Display of an Economic System (Complete)

(1) **Why is an economic system important?**

o An economic system is important because it functions to produce, distribute, and consume goods and services.

(2) **What are the activities associated with economics?**

o General Activities
- an economic system is established
- government oversees economic activity
- economic system interacts internationally

o Production Activities
- land, labor, capital, and management are used to establish production or service facilities
- a good is manufactured or a service is developed

o Distribution Activities
- good or service is marketed
- good is shipped or service is made available

o Consumption Activities
- supply and demand determines the price of goods and services
- consumers shop for goods and services

(3) **What are some consequences of economics?**

Positive consequences: If an economic system succeeds, then individuals and society can produce and raise the standard of living.

Negative consequences: If an economic system fails, then individuals and society will suffer and have a lower or poor standard of living.

(4) **What persons, places, things, and ideas (resources) are associated with economics?**

o land, labor, capital, management	o consumers, workers o unions
o labor unions	o Money, banking, and financial system
o entrepreneurs / businesses	o government

Vocabulary Box

economic system: an operating system for production, distribution, and consumption of goods and services (for example: capitalism, socialism, or communism)

standard of living: the quantity and quality of goods and services available to individuals or society.

land: natural resources and physical property, *Labor:* human effort, *Capital:* machinery, *management:* overall coordination of production efforts

good: a tangible item (e.g. a tablet personal computer), *service:* a process (e.g. a haircut)

ECONOMISTS

Assignment 1—The Job of an Economist

Read the job description of economists in Text Box 7.3.

Text Box 7.3

JOB TITLE: ECONOMIST

Economists study the ways a society distributes scarce resources, such as land, labor, raw materials, and machinery. These resources are used to produce goods and services. Economists study the production and distribution of resources, goods, and services by collecting and analyzing data, researching trends, and evaluating economic issues. They design policies or make recommendations for solving economic problems.

Economists apply economic analysis to issues within a variety of fields, such as education, health, development, and the environment. Some economists study the cost of products, health care, or energy. Others examine employment levels, business cycles, exchange rates, taxes, inflation, or interest rates. Economists often study historical trends and use them to make forecasts. They research and analyze data using a variety of software programs, including spreadsheets, statistical analysis, and database management programs.

Many economists work in federal, state, and local government. Federal government economists collect and analyze data about the U.S. economy, including employment, prices, productivity, and wages, among other types of data. Economists working for corporations help them understand how the economy will affect their business so it may maximize its profits. Economists also work for research firms and think tanks, where they study and analyze a variety of economic issues.

Assignment 2—The Job of an Economist

Prepare a three-stage MG1 subject matter display based on the material in Assignment 1. Title your display A Subject Matter Display of Economists. Be sure to group and title related activities. Write the display in your notebook.

Teacher Resources

1. As a homework assignment, have students research careers at http://www.bls.gov/ooh/home.htm. Students select a career, read about it, and develop a three-stage MG1 subject matter display.
2. As a homework assignment, and based on the career selected in item 1, have students develop the resources they will need to prepare themselves for the career.

Students group the resources per itechniques 18, 19, and 20 as described in Chapter 3, Mind Grammar Instructional Techniques.

THE DECLARATION OF INDEPENDENCE

Assignment 1—Obtain a Copy of the Declaration of Independence

Obtain and read a copy of the Declaration of Independence by (a) visiting a library; (b) obtaining a copy of *The Citizen's Almanac* (2014), U.S. Department of Homeland Security, Washington, DC; or (c) visiting http://www.archives.gov/exhibits/charters/declaration_transcript.html.

Assignment 2—Identify the Intent (the Objective) of the Declaration of Independence

Read the Declaration again. What do you think is its main purpose (i.e., its objective)? Write a complete sentence in your notebook.

Assignment 3—Develop a Three-Stage MG1 Subject Matter Display

Apply MG1 critical reading to the Declaration and develop a three-stage MG1 subject matter display. Account for each activity in the Declaration. Group similar activities. Develop a heading for each group and enter the headings in the display.

Here is an example of an approach that uses three main headings: (a) The King of Great Britain is destructive because he; (b) The Thirteen Colonies, in response, have; and (c) The Colonies, therefore, declare that. *Note:* The letters *a*, *b*, and *c* are used here for purposes of clarification. They do not need to appear in your display.

You may choose to use different and additional headings. Include examples of activities under each main heading that you use.

Assignment 4—Identify the Consequences within the Declaration

Find the consequences within the Declaration. Then update your MG1 display to an MG2 display by adding the consequences. You may also add consequences that do not appear in the Declaration but which you think are important.

Teacher Resources

1. Here are references for the Declaration of Independence: (a) *The Citizen's Almanac* (2014), U.S. Department of Homeland Security, Washington, DC, p. 48. (b) The Declaration may also be found at http://www.archives.gov/exhibits/charters/declaration_transcript.html.
2. The subject matter display shown here in Figure 7.4 contains material that represents answers to Assignments 2, 3, and 4. It does not represent a single correct answer. Figure 7.4 may be distributed to students after assignments have been completed.

Figure 7.4

Title: A Four-Stage MG2 Subject Matter Display of
The United States Declaration of Independence—Adopted on July 4, 1776

(1) **Purpose (What purpose does the Declaration address?)**
o The purpose of the United States Declaration of Independence is to "throw off" the existing government by declaring economic and political independence from Great Britain.

(2) **Activities (What main actions appear in the Declaration?)**
o The King of Great Britain is destructive through "repeated injuries and usurpation's" including:
- refusal to "Assent to Laws" developed by the Colonies
- suspension of ability for each Colony to elect representatives
- quartering of troops
- town burnings
- no jury trials
- no trade
- taxes without consent

o The Thirteen Colonies, in response, have:
- petitioned the King of Great Britain for redress of our grievances
- warned, reminded, and appealed to our "British Brethren" of our tyrannical circumstances
- King and Brethren have ignored us, we now "hold them . . . Enemies in War, in Peace, Friends"

o The Colonies, therefore, declare that:
- "these . . . Colonies are . . . free and independent states"
- all political bonds with Great Britain are dissolved
- we assume equal station with other independent states
- "we mutually pledge to each other our Lives, our Fortunes, and our sacred Honor"

(3) **Consequences** (What consequences followed from the Declaration?)
Positive for United States: Establishment of the unalienable rights to life, liberty, and the pursuit of happiness; ability to self-govern. Long-term: Elimination of slavery, the United States became the prime example of a democracy, Grèat Britain became a great ally.
Positive for Great Britain: Long-term: USA became a great ally
Negative for United States: The Revolutionary War, loss of lives. Long term: a nation divided by the aftereffects of slavery.
Negative for Great Britain: The Revolutionary War, loss of lives, diminished empire.

(4) **Resources** (What person, places, things, and ideas are mentioned in the Declaration?)

o nature's God		o laws of nature	o truths (all men created equal)	
o 56 U. S. representatives		o people	o King of Great Britain's Government	
o injuries	o troops	o towns	o jury	o trials
o trade	o taxes	o lives	o fortunes	o honor

Notes: (1) Not all activities in the Declaration are shown. (2) Only the first U.S. positive consequence appears in the Declaration. (3) For a discussion of subject matter displays based on rhetoric-loaded material, see the heading How to Tell if a Display Based on Rhetoric-Loaded Material is Acceptable, in Chapter 4.

Vocabulary Box:
Self-Evident - obvious and understandable
Tyranny - arbitrary exercise of power
Dissolve - to separate into parts

CREDIT INFORMATION AGENCIES

Assignment 1—Make This List Logical

The function of a credit information agency is to provide a seller with information on the creditworthiness of a potential customer. Figure 7.5 contains a list of related activities. The underlined entries represent headings for groups of activities. The three headings are in order. However, the eight activities may not belong or may be out of order where they appear in Figure 7.5. Relocate as necessary and place the activities in logical order under each heading.

Figure 7.5

Out-of-Order Credit Activities

On the Part of the Potential Customer
o answers questions
o produces confidential reports for use by seller

On the Part of the Seller
o reviews credit application
o checks references
o collects data

On the Part of the Credit Information Agencies
o fills out credit application
o checks with a credit information agency
o Based on reports, rejects or approves credit application in compliance with laws

Assignment 2—Develop a Subject Matter Display

Based on the information in Assignment 1 and your reordered list of activities, develop a three-stage MG1 display.

Assignment 3—Identify Consequences for Seller and Potential Customer

For both the seller and the potential customer, identify positive consequences if the function of the credit information agency *is* performed properly. For both the seller and the potential customer, identify negative consequences if the function of the credit information agency *is not* performed properly.

Teacher Resources

The subject matter display shown in Figure 7.6 contains material that represents answers to Assignments 1, 2, and 3. It does not represent a single correct answer. Figure 7.6 may be distributed to students after assignments have been completed.

Figure 7.6

Title: A Four-Stage MG2 Subject Matter Display of Credit Information Agencies

(1) **What is the function of a credit information agency?**
o The function of a credit information agency is to provide a seller with information on the credit-worthiness of a potential customer.

(2) **What takes place?**

Potential Customer
o fills out credit application
o answers questions

Seller
o reviews credit application
o checks with a credit information agency
o checks references
o Based on reports, rejects or approves credit application in compliance with laws

Credit Information Agencies
o collects data
o produces confidential reports for use by seller

(3) **Consequences (What can happen if function is performed?)**
Positive (if credit information agency's function *is* performed properly): (1) Seller can make proper decision regarding potential customer's credit-worthiness. (2) Potential customer will receive credit to make purchasing of goods and services easier. (3) Seller will have higher sales and fewer defaults.
Negative (if credit information agency's function *is not* performed properly): (1) Potential customer can overextend financially and cannot pay bills. (2) Seller has receivables that are not collectable.

(4) **Resources** (persons, places, things, ideas)

o customer	o seller	
o credit application	o credit agencies	o credit laws

ADDITIONAL TEACHER RESOURCES

Here are several subject matter displays on a variety of topics. They may be used as the basis for designing classroom assignments and assembling them into an instructional set. Use them to design classroom assignments by pairing them, as you see fit, with the instructional techniques discussed in Chapter 3.

Subject Matter Display of Bloom's Taxonomy of Educational Objectives—Book I Cognitive Domain

In Figure 7.7 on Bloom's Taxonomy, note the extended treatment of consequences. Also, note the list of references that support the statements made.

Figure 7.7

Title: A Three Stage MG2 Subject Matter Display of
Bloom's Taxonomy of Educational Objectives - Book I Cognitive Domain

(1) **Purpose of the Taxonomy**

o The purpose of Bloom's Taxonomy is to classify the goals of our educational system. [Note: Bloom stated his *committee's* intent as "It is intended to provide for classification of the goals of our educational system" [Bloom, et al, 1956, p. 1].

(2) **What Activities Led to the Taxonomy?**

o The Taxonomy Committee gathered a long list of educational objectives from educational institutions and the literature.

o The entries were analyzed and grouped by what they had in common.

o All the groups were synthesized and a hierarchy of six levels of cognition was classified as follows.

The Hierarchy of Cognitive Operations [Bloom, et al, 1956, p. 18]

1. Knowledge is the recall of specific information as well as recall of methods and processes.
2. Comprehension is the knowledge and use of information in a communication.
3. Application is the ability to use ideas, rules, theories, and methods.
4. Analysis is the systematic breakdown of the component elements in communication.
5. Synthesis is to form a whole by assembling its associated parts.
6. Evaluation is making qualitative and quantitative value judgments concerning resources and processes used for a given purpose.

o Educational goals associated with the six levels of cognition were then developed and published.

(3) **The Consequences of the *Taxonomy***

Positive Consequences of the Taxonomy:

- Provides a good basis for writing test items, opened up a still ongoing discussion on the proper order of the levels of thinking, provides a framework for preparing standards, and used by some instructors in an attempt to engage students in higher-level questioning,

- Provided a basis for others to reconsider alternative views and approaches to such taxonomy. But none deal with the basic cognitive disconnect inherent in the hierarchy. In this connection, see Anderson, et al. (2001), Hess et al (2009), Marzano and Kendall (2007), and Webb (in Hess, 2009). All offer variations on Bloom's taxonomic scheme, but they do offer an underlying reasoning strategy and do not contest Bloom's placement of comprehension before analysis, synthesis, and evaluation.

Negative Consequences of the Taxonomy:

- The Taxonomy is not based on an identified or developed reasoning theory upon which to base its cognitive hierarchy [Bloom, et al, 1956, p. 17]. Therefore, the Committee operated without a theory of subject matter or a theory of critical thinking. See, Bloom's Dilemma, in *Fixing Instruction*, page 57.

- The hierarchy places comprehension below analysis, synthesis, and evaluation. But, mind grammar shows that comprehension can only be achieved by first engaging in analysis, synthesis, and evaluation [Maiorana, *Fixing Instruction*, 2016, Figure 3.1, p. 61].

- The hierarchy's ordering may account for a cognitive disconnect. This is the mistaken and widely-held belief that one must already know about a topic before one can analyze, synthesize and evaluate (think critically) about that topic.

- Although the Taxonomy is still part of teacher preparation programs, it does not inform effectively the practice of instructors. According to Anderson (1994), teachers are aware of Bloom's Taxonomy. However, they do not make routine use of it in the context of explaining subject matter. Anderson found that according to researchers, teachers ask many questions. Most of the questions oblige students to recall subject matter content rather than think, read, and write of it critically. In addition, these findings seem to be consistent whether considering course content, grade levels, students' ages, ability levels, or countries. See *Fixing Instruction*, Chapters 2 through 6 for the impact of serialism-based instruction.

References

Anderson, L. W., Krathwohl, D. R., Airasian, P. W., Cruikshank, K. A., Mayer, R. E., Pintrich, P. R., Raths, J., and Wittrock, M. C. (2001). *A Taxonomy for Learning, Teaching, and Assessing*. New York: Longman.

Anderson, L. W. (1994). Research on teaching and teacher education. In L. W. Anderson and L. A. Sosniak (eds.), *Bloom's Taxonomy of Educational Objectives—A Forty-Year Retrospective, Ninety-Third Yearbook of the National Society for the Study of Education* (pp. 126–45). Chicago, IL: The University of Chicago Press.

Bloom, B. S., Engelhart, M. D., Furst, E. J., Hill, W. H., and Krathwohl, D. R. (eds.) (1956). *Taxonomy of Educational Objectives: The Classification Of Educational Goals. Handbook I:Cognitive domain*. New York: David McKay.

Hess, K. K., Carlock, D., Jones, B., and Walkup, J. R. (2009). What exactly do "fewer, clearer, and higher standards" really look like in the classroom? Using a cognitive rigor matrix to analyze curriculum, plan lessons, and implement assessments. Retrieved from http://schools.nyc.gov/NR/rdonlyres/D106125F-FFF0-420E-86D9-254761638C6F/0/HessArticle.pdf.

Maiorana, V.P. (2016). *Fixing instruction - Resolving major issues with a core body of knowledge for critical instruction*. Lanham, MD: Rowman & Littlefield.

Marzano, R. J. and Kendall, J. S. (2007). The New Taxonomy of Educational Objectives, 2nd ed. Thousand Oaks, CA: Corwin Press.

A Subject Matter Display of Maslow's Theory of Human Needs

Figure 7.8

Title: A Two-Stage MG1 Subject Matter Display of
Maslow's Theory of Human Needs

(1) **What is the End-in-View of Maslow's Theory of Human Needs?**
o The end-in-view of Maslow's theory of human needs is to show that human beings are driven to think and act in ways that fulfill basic needs.

(2) **What are the Means (conditions, processes, actions, operations) that produce the end-in-view?**
o humans first fulfill basic needs such as that for food, shelter, and safety
o they go on to fulfill needs for belongingness, love, and self-esteem
o humans then self-actualize to meet the need for self-fulfillment

A Subject Matter Display of a Typical American Business

Figure 7.9

Title: A Two-Stage MG1 Subject Matter Display of a
Typical American Business

(1) **The Purpose of a Typical American Business**
The purpose of a typical American Business is to make a profit.

(2) **The Main Activities in a Typical American Business**
o identify a product or service to sell
o obtain financing
o hire and train employees
o produce a product or provide a service
o market product or service
o process business data
o manage the company

A Subject Matter Display of Martin Luther King Jr.'s "I Have a Dream" Speech

Figure 7.10

Topic: A Four-Stage MG2 Subject Matter display of
Martin Luther King Jr.'s "I Have a Dream" Speech

(1) **End-in-View** (What is the end-in-view of Dr. King's Speech?)
o The end-in-view of the speech is to demonstrate for freedom, dramatize a shameful condition, and to remind America of the fierce urgency of now.

(2) **Activities** (The activities that are cited in the speech?)
Introduction
o Emancipation Proclamation signed 100 years ago
o but Negro still not free.
o Declaration of Independence guaranteed life, liberty, and pursuit of happiness
o but America has defaulted on promise, should make real the promise of democracy
o discontent will not pass, but must not be guilty of wrongful deeds, must not distrust all white people
o will never be satisfied until justice rolls like mighty stream soul force
Description of dream
o people will sit in brotherhood, Mississippi will be oasis of freedom and justice
o my children judged by character, not color, black and white children will hold hands in Alabama
o all places made good, we shall all see God's glory
The Future
o I will go back to the South with the hope / faith of dream, we will persevere
o know that one day we will be free, will be able to sing with new meaning "My country, 'tis of thee..."

(3) **Consequences** (What can happen if dream is realized/unrealized?)

Positive (If dream is realized): All people will join hands and sing: "Free at last, free at last; thank God almighty, we are free at last." Freedom will ring.

Negative (If dream is not realized): Continued strife and suffering.

(4) **Resources** (What persons, places, things, and ideas does the speech cite?)

o MLK Jr.	o you	o A. Lincoln o Declaration of Independence			
o Emancipation Proclamation		o America o nation's capital			
o democracy	o US Constitution	o citizens of color		o God's children	o white people
o citizenship rights	o freedom and justice		o suffering	o biracial army	o places in America
o Mississippi	o hope o children	o faith	o Alabama	o Negro spiritual	o God's glory
o The South	o freedom				

Reference: Washington, J. M. (Ed.) (1986). *A Testament of Hope—The Essential Writings of Martin Luther King, Jr.* San Francisco: Harper and Row, pp. 217-220.
Comment: The speech is 1555 words long. There are 352 words in the above study. As with the Gettysburg Address, or any speech, no paper and pencil study can evoke the time, place, atmosphere,

APPLICATION ASSIGNMENTS

The assignments below call for the design of instructional sets. Develop a four-stage MG2 subject matter display (or its mind grammar equivalent) as the basis for designing the set's classroom assignments. When designing the classroom assignments within a set, (1) select or adapt the instructional techniques from those given in Chapter 3 or create your own original instructional techniques; (2) include at least three assignments in each set; and (3) engage students in some combination of thinking, reading/speaking, writing/listening, and observing for critical understanding and/or comprehension using the MG1 and/or MG2 reasoning strategy of your choice.

1. [Teaching]

Develop a subject matter display on the topic of teaching from the teacher's point of view. Group your activities by name. The first group name should be Preparation for Instruction. Be sure your display addresses (a) instructional reasoning strategies for engaging subject matter and (b) positive and negative consequences from the viewpoints of teacher-preparation programs, teachers, students, and parents. Then develop an instructional set based on your display.

2. [The Lesson Plan]

Instructional practice in the form of classroom assignments is the most important part of a lesson plan. Therefore, when developing your display be sure to emphasize the design of classroom assignments. Also, be sure to address the reasoning strategy or strategies on which the classroom assignments are based. Develop an instructional set based on your display. *Note:* For a discussion of thinking strategies that can provide the basis for classroom assignments, see Chapter 3, Thinking: The First Language Art, in *Preparation for Critical Instruction* (Maiorana, 2016b).

3. [Critical Explanation]

Develop an instructional set on critical explanation.

4. [Instruction]

Develop an instructional set on critical instruction.

5. [Instructional Set]

For question 4 in Chapter 2, you developed a four-stage MG2 subject matter display of the instructional set. Use the display as the basis to develop an instructional set on the instructional set.

6. [Assessing Instructional Practice]

Develop an instructional set on assessing instructional practice.

7. [Learning]

Develop a display on the topic of learning from the student's point of view. Be sure your subject matter display addresses reasoning strategies. Then develop an instructional set based on your display.

8. [Testing]

Develop an instructional set on testing. You decide the point of view.

9. [Bloom's Taxonomy]

Use Figure 7.7, Bloom's Taxonomy of Educational Objectives—Book I Cognitive Domain, and develop an instructional set.

10. [Hierarchy of Cognitive Operations]

You may have your own view of the hierarchy of cognitive operations shown in the activities portion of the subject matter display in Figure 7.7. You may wish to add, delete, or reorder how the mind deals with subject matter. Settle on an order and create a three-stage MG2 subject matter display. Then design an instructional set with assignments that take students up through the hierarchy.

11. [The Constitution of the United States]

Develop a display on the Constitution of the United States. Then use that display to design an instructional set. For guidelines on how to treat the activities mentioned in the Constitution, see Assignment 3 in the instructional set on the Declaration of Independence. For a copy of the Constitution of the United States, (a) visit a library, (b) visit https://www.uscis.gov and use search term M-654, or (c) Google M-654.

12. [Maslow's Theory of Human Needs]

Use the subject matter display in Figure 7.8, Maslow's Theory of Human Needs, and develop an instructional set.

13. [Typical American Business]

Use the subject matter display in Figure 7.9, Typical American Business, and develop an instructional set.

14. [Accounting]

Develop an instructional set that addresses Generally Accepted Accounting Principles.

15. [Marketing]

Develop an instructional set on the topic of marketing.

16. [Anthropologist]

Develop an instructional set on the job of an anthropologist. For information, visit http://www.bls.gov/ooh/life-physical-and-social-science/anthropologists-and-archeologists.htm.

17. [Martin Luther King Jr.'s "I Have a Dream" Speech]

Use the subject matter display in Figure 7.10, Martin Luther King Jr.'s "I Have a Dream" speech, and develop an instructional set.

18. [History]

Select a chapter from a history textbook, apply MG2 reading strategy to the material, and develop an instructional set. For an example of how to develop a subject matter display for a textbook chapter, see Text Box 7.17, How to Summarize a Textbook Chapter for Critical Comprehension, in *Preparation for Critical Instruction* (Maiorana, 2016b)

19. [Language]

As a language teacher, you want to show your students how to use proper nouns in the language you teach. The subject matter display you develop will be in English except that the specific examples you provide within the display will be in the language you teach. Use your display to develop an instructional set. For an example of a display and a set based on a grammar topic, see the set on The Adverb in Chapter 4. For another example of a display on a grammar topic, see Figure 4.10 on the comma.

20. [Sports]

Develop an instructional set on your favorite sport. When developing consequences, be sure to consider the players, fans, coaches, and owners.

BIBLIOGRAPHY

Anderson, L. W. (1994). Research on teaching and teacher education. In L. W. Anderson & L. A. Sosniak (Eds.), *Bloom's taxonomy of educational objectives: A forty-year retrospec-*

tive, ninety-third yearbook of the National Society for the Study of Education (pp. 126–145). Chicago, IL: The University of Chicago Press.

Anderson, L. W., Krathwohl, D. R., Airasian, P. W., Cruikshank, K. A., Mayer, R. E., Pintrich, P. R., . . . Wittrock, M. C. (2001). *A taxonomy for learning, teaching, and assessing*. New York, NY: Longman.

Bloom, B. S., Engelhart, M. D., Furst, E. J., Hill, W. H., and Krathwohl, D. R. (Eds.). (1956). *Taxonomy of educational objectives: The classification of educational goals: Handbook I: Cognitive domain*. New York, NY: David McKay.

Bureau of Labor Statistics. (2015a). *Occupational outlook handbook*. Retrieved from http://www.bls.gov/ooh/home.htm

Bureau of Labor Statistics. (2015b). *Occupational outlook handbook: Anthropologists and archeologists*. Retrieved from http://www.bls.gov/ooh/life-physical-and-social-science/anthropologists-and-archeologists.htm

Bureau of Labor Statistics. (2015c). *Occupational outlook handbook: Economists*. Retrieved from http://www.bls.gov/ooh/life-physical-and-social-science/economists.htm

Charters of Freedom. (n.d.). Constitution of the United States. Retrieved from http://www.archives.gov/exhibits/charters/constitution.html

Hess, K. K., Carlock, D., Jones, B., and Walkup, J. R. (2009). What exactly do "fewer, clearer, and higher standards" really look like in the classroom? Using a cognitive rigor matrix to analyze curriculum, plan lessons, and implement assessments. Retrieved from http://schools.nyc.gov/NR/rdonlyres/D106125F-FFF0-420E-86D9-254761638C6F/0/HessArticle.pdf

Maiorana, V. P. (2016a). *Fixing instruction: Resolving major issues with a core body of knowledge for critical instruction*. Lanham, MD: Rowman & Littlefield.

Maiorana, V. P. (2016b). *Preparation for critical instruction: How to explain subject matter while teaching all learners to think, read, and write critically*. Lanham, MD: Rowman & Littlefield.

Marzano, R. J., and Kendall, J. S. (2007). *The new taxonomy of educational objectives* (2nd ed.). Thousand Oaks, CA: Corwin Press.

U.S. Department of Homeland Security. (2014). The Declaration of Independence. *The Citizen's Almanac*. Washington, DC.

Washington, J. M. (Ed.). (1986). *A testament of hope: The essential writings of Martin Luther King, Jr.* San Francisco, CA: Harper & Row.

Glossary

A

Argumentation Argumentation is one mode of critical thinking. It includes the practices of revealing faulty reasoning in another, seeking agreement on a given issue, debating issues, and attempts at persuasion and resolution.

C

Cogeracy Cogeracy is the ability to think recollectively, logically, critically, and creatively.

Core Body of Knowledge for Critical Instruction A typical core body of knowledge includes a common language of practice, foundation principles and skills, and associated standards. For instructional practice, the core includes a language of instruction; teaching and learning standards for critical thinking, reading, and writing; the four categories of thinking; and teacher preparation courses in critical learning and critical instruction.

Critical Comprehension To comprehend a subject matter topic critically is to reveal its objective, the processes that achieve the objective, and the consequences that follow.

Critical Instruction Critical instruction practice is the explicit explanation of how to connect and integrate the objectives, processes, and consequences within subject matter in ways that concurrently develop critical thinking, reading, and writing abilities in all students.

Critical Learning Critical learning is gaining critical comprehension of content while concurrently developing the ability to think, read, and write critically. Critical learning is the basis for critical instruction.

Critical Reading Critical reading for understanding is the application of MG1 mind grammar to textual material. Critical reading for comprehension is the application of MG2 mind grammar to textual material. See questions 9 and 10 under the heading Questions and Answers Regarding Critical Instruction Practice in Chapter 2.

Critical Thinking When discussing critical thinking, one needs to make clear which mode one has in mind. The same applies to the thoughts of others who speak and write of critical thinking. There are three modes of critical thinking: (1) understanding/comprehension/explanation, (2) argumentation, and (3) problem solving.

Within Mode 1, comprehension and its cognitive twin, explanation, are the most important as concerns classroom instruction and learning. They involve the explicit, reliable, and systematic connection and integration of the ideas and facts associated with the intent, processes, and consequences of a given subject matter topic. See question 14 under the heading Questions and Answers Regarding Critical Instruction Practice in Chapter 2.

Critical Understanding To understand a subject matter topic critically is to reveal its objective and the processes that achieve the objective.

Critical Writing for Explanation Critical writing for explanation is the application of MG1 mind grammar to a given topic. Critical writing for comprehension is explanation based on the application of MG2 mind grammar to a given topic. The mind grammar elements can appear in any order, can be mixed, and can be revisited. See questions 11 and 12 under the heading Questions and Answers Regarding Critical Instruction Practice in Chapter 2.

D

Deep Learning There are three levels of deep learning: understanding, comprehension, and pathway development. Achieving deep *understanding* of a given topic requires a first level of critical thinking in the form of MG1 reasoning strategy. MG1 reveals *the topic's* objective and activities. Achieving deep *comprehension* of a given topic requires a second, more thoughtful, level of critical reasoning. Using MG2, this takes the form of revealing *the topic's* objective, activities, and consequences. Pathway development is used to achieve still deeper learning. One uses MG1 or MG2 to address a subtopic within a given topic. See itechniques 73 and 74 in Chapter 3.

Differentiated Instruction Such instruction requires teachers to change their instructional approaches to suit the individual needs of each student in class. With serialism-based instruction, this desired objective is near impossible to achieve. On the other hand, critical instruction does lend itself to a realistic form of differentiated instruction. See the answer to question 7 under the heading Questions and Answers Regarding Critical Instruction Practice in Chapter 2.

I

Instructional Community There are three parts to the instructional community: immediate, related, and extended. The immediate instructional community includes teacher–educators, teacher-candidates, school and college faculty, counselors, teacher aides, professional developers, parents who homeschool, curriculum and instruction designers, and principals. For more on the instructional community, see endnote 13 in Chapter 1.

Instructional Methodology An instructional methodology is a combination of a specific istrategy and a specific itechnique for *engaging subject matter*. One selects a specific istrategy and merges it with a specific itechnique to form a specific imethod.

Instructional Set Based on Mind Grammar as an Instruction and Learning Strategy An instructional set is a collection of classroom assignments that address a specific subject matter topic. The assignments in a *mind grammar–based* instructional set are founded on the use of mind grammar critical reasoning strategies. Assignments within such a set use instructional techniques, with mind grammar as the instructional strategy. This leads students to not only think critically but to read, listen, write, speak, and observe critically as well.

Instructional Strategy An instructional strategy is the mental view one takes of subject matter. Istrategy is how one reasons when thinking of new and revisited subject matter. An explicit istrategy is *arranging subject matter* according to some *reasoning framework* or thinking theory for purposes of understanding, comprehending, and explaining subject matter.

Instructional Technique An instructional technique provides the means to implement an istrategy. An itechnique is a way to actively engage students *with the subject matter at hand.* All itechniques are used in the context of some explicit istrategy.

L

Logical Thinking Logical thinking is the listing of persons, places, things, and/or ideas in an orderly sequence where the concern is the internal serial logic of the list itself and not the meaning, function, or purpose served by the subject matter of the list.

M

Mind Grammar, Formal Formal mind grammar is the systematic and explicitly critical and patterned way to engage new and revisited subject matter. Formal mind grammar represents an explicit critical thinking strategy for understanding, comprehending, explaining, reading, and writing. Such thinking applies to critically explaining something to one's self (i.e., self-instruction) or to others (i.e., instruction). Based on the way the mind works naturally, MG1 and MG2 mind grammar provide the basis for teachers and students to develop and share explicit critical thinking patterns when thinking, reading, and writing.

Mind Grammar, Informal Informal mind grammar is the innate and informal way the human mind deals with daily life. It generally follows the pattern of intent-activities and, when functioning fully, considers the consequences that follow.

Ordinarily, when it comes to engaging new and revisited subject matter, we do not explicitly and formally use that innate pattern when thinking, reading, and writing.

Mind Grammar 1 (MG1) MG1 is the use of the pattern objective-process when engaging subject matter. MG1 helps all learners (teachers and students) to achieve critical subject matter *understanding* and engage in critical reading and writing.

Mind Grammar 2 (MG2) MG2 is the use of the pattern objective-process-consequences when engaging subject matter. MG2 helps all learners (teachers and students) to achieve critical subject matter comprehension and engage in critical reading and writing.

Modes of Critical Thinking See *Critical Thinking*.

N

New and Revisited Subject Matter New subject matter refers to curriculum content that is new to the K through graduate learner. Revisited subject matter refers to previously discussed content that the learner has not grasped or reviewing content for purposes of reinforcement or test preparation.

P

Pathway Development Depth of learning on a given topic never really ends. Critical thinking for deeper comprehension can begin anew by investigating subtopics associated with a main topic. Seeking deeper comprehension of a subtopic related to a given topic is called pathway development. Developing pathways to deepen comprehension can be repeated for any subtopic and its subtopics. This continues until the learner has reached a level of comprehension that suits his or her needs. See the topic heading Pathways to Still Deeper Learning in Chapter 4, p. 52, in *Preparation for Critical Instruction: How to Explain Subject Matter While Teaching All Learners to Think, Read, and Write Critically* (Maiorana, 2016b).

Pedagogical Content Knowledge Content knowledge is what one knows about a subject. Pedagogical content knowledge (PCK) refers to the instructional skills needed to teach that subject. In the education culture, the use of the PCK term is misleading. It implies that the disciplines are markedly different structurally. Therefore, each discipline requires its own unique way of instruction to promote understanding and comprehension. The practice of critical instruction shows that this is not true.

Critical thinking, reading, and writing in the form of mind grammar apply to all disciplines. It is universal and not unique to any discipline. Therefore, it is more realistic to say that PCK refers to certain in-discipline truisms, issues, problems, and approaches to problem solving that experience shows lend themselves to effective instruction. For more on this, see *Fixing Instruction: Resolving Major Issues with a Core Body of Knowledge for Critical Instruction* (Maiorana, 2016a), Chapter 3.

Problem Solving Problem solving is one mode of critical thinking. It addresses situations that require resolution. Approaches to problem solving include the problem-solving method, the decision-making process, and the scientific method.

S

Serialism-Based Instruction Serialism-based instruction is the discussion of subject matter topics one after another without also making and revealing critical connections within and among the topics. Because it provides no critical pattern for subject matter engagement, serialism-based instruction induces rote learning and defeats the concurrent development of critical thinking, reading, and writing abilities.

Serialism Strategy Serialism strategy is the strictly linear and traditional mental view of subject matter. It reveals little with respect to how all subject matter is universally and critically constructed, connected, and integrated.

Subject Matter Subject matter is anything that you can think about. Subject matter is anything you can read, write, and talk about or hear and observe. Subject matter is anything you can sense or the mind can imagine. Subject matter is anything in this world and beyond. For more on the nature of subject matter, see the reference given in endnote 7 in Chapter 1.

Subject Matter Objective A subject matter objective is a complete statement of the intent or end-in-view, effect, meaning, purpose, function, or importance of the *subject matter topic* at hand.

Subject Matter Universals All subject matter is composed of the ideas, concepts, theories, facts, and processes ever discovered, conceived, imagined, revealed, believed, and thought of by the human mind. These elements take the systematic form of intent (i.e., objective), processes, and consequences. This pattern is universal in all curriculum subject matter, the product of the human mind. Accordingly, regardless of discipline, all subject matter topics share this common systematic theme. It is through formal mind grammar that the universal elements of subject matter are revealed critically.

BIBLIOGRAPHY

Maiorana, V. P. (2016a). *Fixing instruction: Resolving major issues with a core body of knowledge for critical instruction.* Lanham, MD: Rowman & Littlefield.

Maiorana, V. P. (2016b). *Preparation for critical instruction: How to explain subject matter while teaching all learners to think, read, and write critically.* Lanham, MD: Rowman & Littlefield.

Index

achievement:
limitations of rote learning and, 27;
reading and, 29, 30, 33;
reasoning strategy and, 5;
thinking, creative, and, 53, 143;
thinking, critical, and. *See* critical thinking;
writing and, 30, 31, 33
argumentation. *See* critical thinking
assignments, classroom:
assessment of, 25;
blended classes and, 29;
core body of knowledge and, xix;
design of, 21;
duration of, 23;
English language learners, and, xxvii, 10, 26, 29, 37, 46;
instructional sets and, 16;
lesson plans and, 16, 35n1;
mind grammar-based, consequences of, 10;
number of in instructional set, 23;
professional practice and, 16;
selecting itechniques for, 24;
special education students, and, 28, 47;
types of, 22;
writing style and, 23

classroom:
assignments. *See* assignments, classroom;
critical instruction, and. *See* critical instruction;
critical thinking, and. *See* critical thinking;
English language arts and, xxv, xxvii, 61;
instructional sets and, 21;
practice, essence of, 15, 16
cogeracy:
categories of, 9;
description of, xxv, 9, 13n14, 143
comprehension:
argumentation and problem solving, and, 7-8;
consequences and, 6;
critical reading and, 74-75;
critical thinking and, 8, 9;
critical writing and, 76;
deep learning and, 144;
everyday life and, 6;
explanation and, xxvi, 7, 9;
patterns, display for, 6, 18;
reasoning strategies for, 4, 8;
understanding, relation to, 6, 7
consequences:
critical comprehension, 6;
critical instruction, 8, 10;
critical learning, 8, 10;
critical thinking, 74, 75;
daily life and, 6, 64;
description of, 21, 64;
examples of, 64;
explanation and, 7;
human mind and, xix, 29, 32;
instruction and, 9;
instructional sets, of, xxvi, 34;
mind grammar and, 6, 7, 18, 145;
mind grammar based assignments, 10;

negative, 21;
positive, 21;
reading for comprehension, 75;
serialism, of, 27;
subject matter universals, and, 5;
what-if questions and, 53;
writing for explanation, 76
core body of knowledge, instructional:
classroom assignments and, xix;
description of, 143;
elements of, xxv;
establishment of, xxv, 12n1;
expansion of, xxv;
lack of in conventional practice, 26, 26, 123n1;
standards and, 143
critical instruction:
classrooms assignments, and. *See* assignments, classroom;
critical learning, and, 10;
description of, xxv, 10;
imethods, and, 4;
istrategy, and, 3;
itechniques, and, 4, 37;
operational basis for, xxvi;
Q&A regarding, 26-34
critical learning:
basis for, 6, 18;
description of, 10, 143;
introducing students to, 26, 36n8, 38, 65, 66;
mind grammar and, 8;
reasoning basis for, 7;
students and, 28
critical observing, 45
critical reading, 8, 29, 30, 32, 43, 75, 96, 143
critical listening, 45, 91
critical thinking:
argumentation and, 7-9, 32, 143;
cognitive waves and, 52;
democratic society and, 11;
descriptions of, 7, 9;
formal and explicit need for, xix, xx, 10, 15, 18;
gift, human, xix, xx, 27;
grammar of mind, xix, xxv, 26, 27, 32;
informal ability and, xix, xx, xxv;
innateness of, xix–xxi, xxv, xxviii;
intent and, xix, 6, 7, 9, 29, 32, 56;
MG1, and. *See* mind grammar one;
MG2, and. *See* mind grammar two;
modes and nature of, 7, 8, 9, 12, 13n7;
pathways and. *See* pathways;
problem solving and, 7–9, 13n11, 32, 49, 144, 147;
purposes of, 7, 9;
questioning and, 32, 52, 53;
reading and, 7, 8, 10, 18, 29, 30, 75;
reasoning strategies for. *See* mind grammar one and two;
standards for, xxv, 34, 36n13, 143;
subject matter, and. *See* subject matter;
subject matter objective and. *See* subject matter objective;
writing and, 7, 8, 10, 18, 30, 31, 76

deep learning:
comprehension and, 6, 7;
description of, 144;
itechniques and, 37, 52;
topics and, 28;
levels of, 144;
pathways for. *See* pathways

explanation:
basis for, 9;
consequences and, 7;
critical explanation, 7;
critical instruction, and, 10;
critical thinking, and, 9;
describing versus explaining, 7;
description, instructional, 18;
graphic organizers, weakness of, 7;
logical thinking, and, 28;
MG1, and, 18;
MG2, and, 18;
most important element of, 5;
reading and, 29;
shared thinking patterns and, 29;
topic selection, and, 17

instruction:
community of, 9, 11, 13n13;
critical. *See* critical instruction;
differentiated, 11, 29, 144
instructional sets:
assembling, 24;
assessing, 25;

classroom assignments in. *See* assignments, classroom;
consequences of, 34;
description of, xx, 16;
developing, procedure for, 16;
end-in-view of, 15;
lesson plans, and, 16, 35n1;
number of assignments in, 23;
reasoning strategy for, 17, 18;
revising, 25;
subject matter display and, 18;
topic selection, 17;
using, 24
instructional terms:
cogeracy, xxv, 9, 13n14;
comprehend, 6;
critical instruction, 10;
critical learning, 10;
critical thinking, 7, 9;
explain, 7;
instructional method, 4, 5;
instructional strategy, 3, 4;
instructional technique, 4, 5;
mind grammar, 6;
subject matter, 5;
subject matter universals, 5;
understand, 6

learning:
critical. *See* critical learning;
deep. *See* deep learning

knowledge. *See* core body of knowledge, instructional

method:
definition, instructional, 4;
examples, instructional, 5
mind grammar:
daily life and, 6, 33;
description of, 6, 145;
English language learners and, 29;
formal, 145;
human mind, and, 5, 18, 26, 35n3, 146;
informal, 145-146;
instructional practice and, 6, 16;
itechniques and, 37;
MG1, 6, 8, 18, 21, 28, 37, 146;
MG2, 6, 8, 18, 21, 28, 37, 146;
nature of, 5, 6, 146;
origination of, 36n6;
special education students and, 28;
subject matter display and, 18;
subject matter narrative and, 19, 31;
subject matter universals and, 5;
vocabulary, 55

objectives:
behavioral, 20;
educational, xxviii, 125, 135, 136;
learning, 20, 35n1.
See also subject matter objectives

pathways:
comprehension and, 146;
deeper learning and, 52;
development of, 146
pedagogical content knowledge, 146
preparation. *See* teacher preparation
problem solving. *See* critical thinking
professional practice:
conventional, 26;
critical instruction and, xix, 6, 26;
essence of, 9;
foundation for. S*ee* core body of knowledge, instructional;
key terms and concepts, 3;
professional development and, xx, xxvi, xxviii, 8;
recognition of, xxi;
responsibilities of, general, 34;
responsibility of, unique, 12;
self-defeating foundation for, 26;
weak conventional foundation for, 26, 27

questions/questioning:
framing, 52, 53;
Bloom's taxonomy and, 136;
conventional nature of, 136;
subject matter and, 32;
critical reasoning and, 32;
mind grammar, and, 32

reading:
close, limitations of, 5, 29;
critical, itechniques for, 43;
critical, istrategies for, 8, 18, 29, 32

serialism and serialism-based instruction:
limitations of, 4, 7, 17, 26;
rote learning and, 26, 27
standards:
core body of knowledge and, 143;
missing, xxv, 36n13
strategy:
definition, instructional, 3;
instructional, examples of, 4;
mind grammar and, 18
students:
achievement as function of teacher practice, xxi;
critical thinking, gift for, xix, xx, 26, 27;
innate abilities of, xix- xxi, 68;
standards, for. *See* standards
subject matter:
composition of, 5;
description of, 5;
display. *See* subject matter display;
equality of, 5;
human mind and, 5;
mind grammar, and, 5;
new and revisited, 13n4;
objectives. *See* subject matter objective;
principles of, xxv;
reasoning strategies, critical. *See* mind grammar;
rhetoric-loaded material and, 73-74;
sources of, 5;
universals, 5, 7, 10, 13n8, 28, 147
subject matter display:
availability of, 19;
blended classes and, 29;
deciding which to use, 28;
developing, 18, 20;
MG1 displays, xx, 18;
MG2 displays, xx, 18;
mind grammar interview and, 32;
most important element of, 5;
narratives and, 19, 28, 31;
pathway development and. *See* pathways;
purpose of, 18;
questions concerning use of, 26;
reasoning strategies for. *See* mind grammar;
reasoning strategy for, 17, 18;
subject matter objective, and. *See* subject matter objective;
title of, 17;
topic for, 17;
translations and, 46;
types of, for comprehension, xxvi, 7, 18;
types of, for understanding, xxvi, 7, 18;
what does not belong in a, 20-21;
word picture and, 18, 26, 62, 67
subject matter displays:
adverb, 69;
American business, 137;
Battle of Gettysburg, 91-92;
Bloom's taxonomy, cognitive domain, 136;
cell phone, 115;
circle, 101;
comma, 77;
Constitution, U.S., first amendment, 127;
counting, 116;
credit information agencies, 135;
critical thinking, three modes of, 74-75;
Declaration of Independence, U.S., 133;
digestive system, 116;
Discurso de Lincoln en Gettysburg, 71-72;
drugs, ethical, 118;
economic system, 129, 130;
electrical batteries, Lunar Module, 119;
electrically charged clouds, 109, 110;
Fauve painting style, 83;
geography, 108;
Herman the horse, 77;
intestine, large, 117;
Jack and Jill, 63;
library (compressed), 79;
Lincoln's Gettysburg Address, 94;
litmus paper, 117;
Martin Luther King Jr.'s "I Have a Dream" Speech, 137-138;
Maslow's theory of human needs, 137;
music, 87, 88;
painting, Andre Derain's *Big Ben*, 86;
perspective, in drawing, 94-95;
philosophy, 95;
probability, 105;
rain (blank), 66;
reading, for critical comprehension, 75;
writing plan, for critical comprehension, 76
subject matter narratives:
adverb, 68;
Discurso Gettysburg De Lincoln, 70;

economist, 131;
First Amendment to the U.S. Constitution, 126, 127;
immunization experiment, 111-112;
Jack and Jill, 61;
Lincoln's Gettysburg Address in English, 92;
Ohm's Law of electricity, 113;
painting, wild style of, 82;
percentages, 102-103;
rain, 65;
subscripted variables, 106
subject matter objective:
alternate views of, 74;
behavioral objectives, vs., 20;
complete statement of, 20;
comprehension, and, 18;
consequences, and, 20, 21;
description of, 5;
dictionaries, and, 50;
forms for, 20;
guidelines for writing, 20;
importance of, 5;
invalid expressions of, 20;
mind grammar activities and, 21;
mind grammar, and, 37;
number of in a display, 20;
students and, 25;
subject matter displays, and, 20;
subject matter universals, and, 5;
understanding, and, 18;
when not readily apparent, 74;
writing a, 20

teachers:
democracy, and, 11, 97;
preparation of. *See* teacher preparation;
professional practice, weak foundation and, 4, 5, 12, 27;
recognition, xxi;
responsibility, essential, 27, 34;
unique responsibility of, 12.
See also professional practice
teacher-candidates. *See* teacher preparation
teacher educators. *See* teacher preparation
teacher preparation:
core body of knowledge. *See* core body of knowledge, instructional;
critical instruction curriculum, xxv;
critical thinking, and, xix, xx, xxv, xxvi, 3, 4, 8;
explaining subject matter, and, 8, 9;
instructional community, and, 13n13;
language of instruction, and, xxv;
professional development. *See* professional practice;
student achievement, and, 5.
See also critical instruction
technique:
instructional, 4;
limitations of, 5;
mind grammar and, 37;
instructional, examples of, 5;
relationship to istrategy and imethod, 5;
underlying instructional strategy and, 5
textbooks:
chapters, critical comprehension of, 44, 57n7;
chapters, critical understanding of, 44, 57n6;
chapters, evaluating a, 44;
displays of subject matter, and, 21;
mind grammar, and, 21;
subject matter treatment, and, 4
thinking:
first language art, 26;
four categories of, xxv, 9.
See also cogeracy; critical thinking

understand:
argumentation and problem solving, and, 8;
comprehension, relation to, 6, 7
consequences and, 6;
critical reading and, 75;
critical thinking and, 8, 9, 74;
critical writing and, 76;
everyday life and, 6;
explanation and, xxvi, 7, 9;
patterns, display for, 6, 18;
reasoning strategies for, 4, 8;

writing:
critical, itechniques for, 42-43;
critical, istrategies for, 8, 18, 29, 32;
critical plan for, 76;
English Language Arts exams and, 30

About the Author

The instructional theories, principles, strategies, and techniques that show how to explain subject matter critically while teaching all learners how to think, read, listen, write, speak, and observe critically are the result of Victor P. Maiorana's original research, development, and practice. His concepts address the universal structure of subject matter and the use of reasoning strategies based on formalizing our innate ability to think critically (referred to as mind grammar). These in turn lead to developing abilities to understand, comprehend, and explain new and revisited subject matter through critical development of the language arts. Taken together, these abilities constitute the basis for critical instruction and critical learning.

His explicit and practical methods for critical instruction represent the antidote to the self-defeating practice of conventional serialism-based instruction. His professional experience with the issue of self-defeating serialism-based instruction and the rote learning it induces began in his first week of college teaching.

He did what many beginning instructors do. For each course, he outlined the first textbook chapter, added some notes based on his experience with the subject matter topic, and then entered the classroom. After the first week he felt very uneasy. All he had done was essentially replay the mind-dulling material as presented in textbooks. He asked himself, "What was I doing for the students that the textbook author was not already doing?" As he was to discover, conventional textbooks treat serially all the facts and ideas within subject matter as if they were on the same mental level. This hides the critical relationships of facts and ideas that are inherent in all subject matter—hence, rote learning.

In the second week, he started an informal research project with his students. Its intent was to find out how students studied their textbooks and how much time they devoted to the activity. The research showed that students simply underlined passages and spent less than three hours per week studying. Eventually, this led to his first book, *How to Learn and Study in College* (1980).

Dr. Maiorana based his doctorate dissertation on an insight he had while writing his first book. The insight revealed the universal and critical nature of all subject matter. This led to his origination of mind grammar for subject matter understanding, comprehension, and explanation. To support this insight, his dissertation committee advised him to examine the writings of others, including John Dewey. The research provided support for Dr. Maiorana's theory of mind grammar and subject matter universals and their application to new and revisited subject matter.

The research won two awards: the 1985 Paul S. Lomax Scholarship and Leadership Award and the 1985 NYU Delta Pi Epsilon Research Award.

Based on his dissertation and classroom application, he next wrote *Critical Thinking Across the Curriculum: Building the Analytical Classroom* (1992). Of this work, the *Journal of Reading* (April 1993) said: "Offers new methodology to counteract the negative effects of older methods [that are] used even by those who teach students preparing to be teachers . . . a valuable method to push critical thinking behaviors into all classrooms for all learners—teachers and students." However, the work was criticized because it did not go far enough in providing theoretical foundations and explicit and practical instructional strategies and techniques.

This led to his *Fixing Instruction: Resolving Major Issues with a Core Body of Knowledge for Critical Instruction* (Rowman & Littlefield, 2016). This work establishes the core knowledge needed for the professional preparation and practice of critical instruction. It establishes the bases for a language of instruction, subject matter universals, mind grammar, standards for thinking, and critical instruction.

A second work, *Preparation for Critical Instruction: How to Explain Subject Matter While Teaching All Learners to Think, Read, and Write Critically* (Maiorana, 2016), expands on the ideas regarding critical teaching and learning introduced in *Fixing Instruction*. To teach critically, one must first know how to learn critically. Therefore, this book is aimed at providing the profession with the theories, principles, and practices for learning critically when engaging new and revisited subject matter. The book formally applies mind grammar reasoning strategies so all learners can think, read, listen, write, and speak critically when engaging new and revisited subject matter in all disciplines.

Both these works have received extensive and extraordinary praise. Please visit www.rowman.com and search by book title. These works set the foundation for practicing critical instruction in the classroom, which brings us to Dr. Maiorana's present book. *Teach Like the Mind Learns: Instruct So Students Learn to Think, Read, and Write Critically* contains descriptions of over ninety mind grammar–based instructional techniques. Many of these itechniques are applied in over twenty-five instructional sets, which are collections of classroom assignments. The sets illustrate the application of mind grammar in the classroom. The sets address topics in the English language arts; the humanities; mathematics, science, engineering, and technology; and the social sciences.